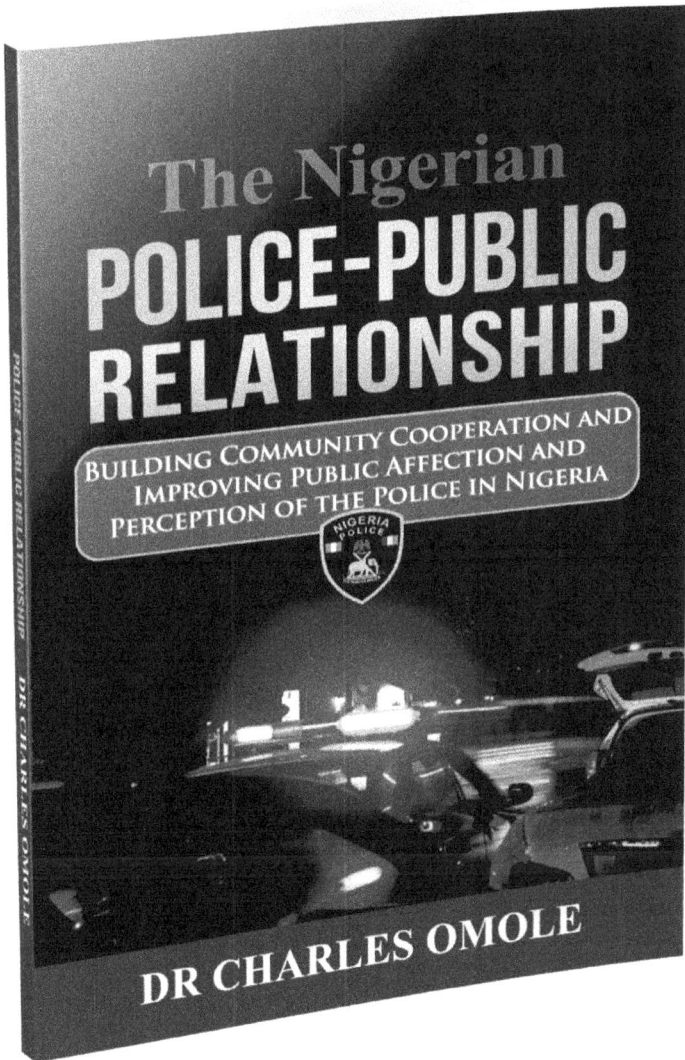

The Nigerian
POLICE-PUBLIC
RELATIONSHIP

BUILDING COMMUNITY COOPERATION AND
IMPROVING PUBLIC AFFECTION AND
PERCEPTION OF THE POLICE IN NIGERIA

DR CHARLES OMOLE

THE NIGERIAN POLICE-PUBLIC RELATIONSHIP

Building Community Cooperation and Improving Public Affection and Perception of the Police in Nigeria

DR CHARLES OMOLE

Copyright 2017
Charles Omole

Published by: Winning Faith

WINNING FAITH

London . New York . Lagos

ISBN: 978-1-907095-28-3

TABLE OF CONTENTS

DEDICATION

The book is dedicated to my late Uncle, who systematically developed my passion for the Nigerian police over many years of his own research and leadership in this field.
Professor Emeritus Tekena N. Tamuno
(28 January 1932 – 11 April 2015)

Your shoes can never be filled but your legacy will continue to inspire us to greater heights.

INTRODUCTION

Trying to shed light on the complex relationship between Nigerians and the police is a challenging and complicated task. Doing so in a book that is concise and abridged is even more difficult. But that is my mission in this book.

I am seeking to explain the causes of the negative perception of the police by Nigerians, tell the police some home truths about their behaviour, enlighten Nigerians about the challenges faced by the police and finally to encourage the rank and file officers who will be reading this book that change is achievable and that there can be light at the end of the current dark tunnel of low morale and disappointments many face.

This could be perceived as the most critical book I have written about the police so far; but I am not a denigrator of the Nigerian police. I love the police and security institutions. I am a fan of the police and I am passionate about helping them become the best in the world.

That is why I have spent years researching and studying their work and why I have committed years to training security and police organisations all over the world.

I will therefore want all the rank and file officers reading this book to relax and not be too defensive. I am your friend. And as friends, I will need to tell you some bitter truth but in the end you will feel better as I will suggest practical ways we can all have the effective police institution we crave in Nigeria.

For a fact, public perception of the police is an essential factor in their willingness to cooperate with the authorities in the fight against crime and criminality. But when the public dislike the police and view them with suspicion and fear; the police has a harder work to do. Regardless of the number of officers employed by the police; it is impossible for the police to be everywhere.

Public perception refers to the conscious understanding that people have of public and official issues or bodies. There may be a basic disparity between the factual truth and the virtual perceived truth influenced by the public opinion and the mass media. Perception is the truth to the public regardless of the reality. And they will act based on their perceptions.

Yet, the support of the general public is crucial to its ability to obtain good intelligence and build better intelligence picture of our communities. Human intelligence is the bedrock of any intelligence led policing effort.

With the historical friction and mistrust between the police and the Nigerian people, cooperation with the police is seen as dangerous as it does not only expose you to reprisals but you could end up becoming the suspect as many have experienced.

There also seem to be an unconcerned attitude to public opinion by the police authorities with many (it seems) are too eager to please their political masters at the expense of public goodwill and perception.

Regardless of the effect or impact of actions taken by the police, the people will support it if they feel the actions are legal, constitutional and ethical. It is the unlawful perception of police actions that makes public trust more difficult to cultivate. Also, the police fondness for underselling their own achievements has exacerbated an already bad situation.

This book is one of the by-products of a detailed three-year research into the Nigerian police. However, as the book is intended for the rank and file officers; it will not be presented as an academic paper.

Instead, the research findings will be mentioned only where necessary but the book will be a practical review of the police-public relationship in Nigeria, causes of the problems and possible solutions for improvement.

We will explore tools needed to bring the police into the modern digital world our Youths live in. How the police can better engage with the communities and more importantly how individual officers must become good ambassadors of the police institution through respect for the public and the rule of law in all they do.

But things are beginning to change little by little. The police authorities have now realized that without the cooperation and support of the people, no amount of officers or budgetary increase will improve their performance.

Changing the Nigerian police will take time, but the work need to start now. The Nigeria Police have some outstanding and brilliant officers (at all ranks), who are sadly caged by a corrupt system and mismanaged institutional framework. I have met many excellent officers in my dealings with the police in Nigeria.

In the coming months and years as these officers rise to the top of the institution, Nigerians will begin to see the obvious transformation needed for better policing in the country. Although the book touches on various topics that deserve detailed treatments, I have endeavoured to keep focused on the purpose of the book so as to avoid an unwieldy and big publication.

This book is intended to help spark the needed debate and champion the creation of the roadmap for an improved public perception of the police and ensure effective community cooperation. Slowly the police are getting some issues right.

I believe Nigerian can be made to love their police. I believe the police can be made an object of affection for Nigerians. I believe a closer relationship can be established between the police and the Nigerian public.

It is my hope that this book will be added to the pool of resources that will help transform and reengineer our police as they begin to win the hearts and mind of Nigerians in the seasons ahead.

The change must indeed begin with you the reader. Yes, we can!

Dr Charles Omole
2017

WISDOM OF A SAGE

"Police must secure the willing COOPERATION OF THE PUBLIC in voluntary observance of the law to be able to secure and maintain the respect of the public."

— **Sir Robert Peel**

CHAPTER ONE

HISTORICAL OVERVIEW OF PUBLIC PERCEPTIONS OF THE POLICE

In governance, perception is greater than reality. It does not matter what you do, it is what people perceive you have done that you are credited with. This is the same with crime reporting all over the world.

The fear of crime indicators tends to be greater than the actual crime figures. So when it comes to the police in Nigeria (as in any country); what the people perceive is more important than what the police think of themselves. In many countries, perception of the police and understanding how the citizens view their police is a constant (possibly yearly) exercise by the police organization and other civic organisations.

But in Nigeria, some argue that such may not be necessary as a national consensus has long be arrived at that puts the Nigeria Police as the most corrupt agency of government in Nigeria.

A report in July 2017 by the government owned National Bureau of Statistics put police as the most corrupt agency of government in Nigeria.[1]

In Nigeria, as in other countries, the police are an agency of government, responsible for the prevention and control of crimes and disorders as well as the detection, apprehension and prosecution of perpetrators of crimes and violence in the country.[2]

---

[1] http://www.nigerianstat.gov.ng/. Accessed on 29 August 2017
[2] Alemika EEO. Colonialism, State and Policing in Nigeria: Crime, Law

Despite this general perception of the police as corrupt and inept, I conducted a three-year research on the Nigerian Police and this book is one of the many publications that highlights the findings with a view to support and transform policing in the nation. In some respect, the public do not understand the plight of the police hence lack empathy for it.

From the start, I must declare my position. I am a patriotic Nigerian and a supporter of the police institution. I am fanatical in my commitment to the transformation of the country and I do not apologise for that.

That is why I am passionate to see the makeover of the police to better serve the Nigerian public in ways we can all be proud of.

So any criticism of the police in this book is done as a critical friend. Friends have to tell each other the truth if change is to be achieved. More so, you cannot change what you do not admit is incorrect. Hence, I have

---

and Social Change. 1993;20:187–219.

dedicated the final Chapter in this book to solutions and remedies based on global best practice.

I also believe that the police organisation has not helped itself or endeared itself to the public through some of its excesses both vicariously through individual bad officers and institutionally through missed opportunities to rebrand and improve its image. We shall be looking at these in details in this and following chapters.

Maintaining the positive image of the police has always been a challenge since the days of the first known police force dating back to the 1800s in Europe.

With the advent of social media, this challenge is amplified exponentially. At a moment's notice, the misdeeds of one officer can go viral across the globe without any ability to mitigate or reconcile the damage.

Part of this is just the cost of doing business in the digital age, but what about the part of the problem that can be influenced by altering human behaviour?

What are the most common daily activities that officers do to fuel a negative image? These are some of the issues that will be discussed in this book.

A salient conclusion from my research is that experiences with the police vary according to department, type of police action, the departmental unit involved and so on.

Perception of the police is therefore a complex subject with responses determined by not only personal experiences of the citizens, but by conventional wisdom, popular myths, rumours and prejudiced or true general public statements by those who may have a beef with the police in the first place.

Historically, the police in Nigeria have always been viewed and characterised as brutal, corrupt and ineffective.[3] This is not a

---

[3] Iwah A. Implementing community policing in Nigeria. In: Abubakar M

new phenomenon at all. But it has progressively gotten worse in the past thirty years it seems. When the colonial authorities merged the Western and Northern Police services to create the Nigeria Police Force (NPF) in 1930; they retained the local or community police constabularies across the country.

These local forces were managed by the surrogates of the colonial masters, local authorities and Obas etc all over the country.

The two forces existed in parallel until 1966 when the Ironsi administration abolished the local forces based on the recommendations of an expert panel set up by the government. Guess why these local forces were abolished? Yes, you guess right, it was due to corruption, nepotism, brutalisation of political opposition and indiscipline.

So as you can see, corruption and public

D. editor. Nigeria Police, the journey so far, Pan African Institute of Para-Legal Studies Abuja, Research and Publication Department, Nigeria; 2013.

outcry against the police has deep colonial roots, thus not just a modern phenomenon.

The police in Nigeria, has actually never really operated based on the consent and cooperation with the citizens. They were imposed on the citizens and seen as tools in the hands of the colonial authorities to oppress and control the locals.

Today, most Nigerians still see the police as a tool by the 'government in power' to oppress the citizens. So, the negative perception problem of the police has been long established as a problem that needs to be fixed.

What the colonial masters failed to do was perpetuated after Independence in 1960. The arrival of Military rule that truncated our democratic experience in the early 1960s, had profound effect on the fate of the police in Nigeria. Initially the police were embraced by the military throughout most of the 1960s because they were needed.

The only organisation that had communication links that covered the entire country was the police. The army, air force or navy did not have such communication links then as they were too small and not well equipped.

So the police were embraced by the military regimes so much so a couple of police leaders were appointed into the governments at that time. Then came the civil war.

After the war, the military was substantially bigger and much better equipped with its own communication links and formations throughout Nigeria. So from the mid-1970s, the military behaved as though police were no longer needed as allies but were seen as tools.

Given that the police were the only legitimate armed organisation that could stop a coup from succeeding; emasculating and weakening the police and making it less effective became the unspoken objective of the military, even though they will not admit to this expressly.

First the Special Branch (intelligence arm of the police) was carved out of the police in the mid 1970s and made into a separate organisation. This was then called the Nigerian Security Organisation (NSO) and then changed to the State Security Service (SSS) of today.

As noted in my book;[4] several other policing related organisation have since been carved out of the police, thus diffusing its funding, cohesion and strength.

As tools in the hands of successive military regimes, the police became more unpopular and hated by Nigerians, who additionally projected their frustrations with the military governments on the police as well.

The security landscape of Nigeria is now littered with about ten civil policing related

---

[4] Omole C. Supporting Good Governance in the Nigerian Police Force – Volume 1. 2016

organisations that are not joined up, with overlapping powers and fragmented.[5]

This historical verdict still prevails today in the minds of the public who do not see the police as their friend but people to be feared and avoided. The unsuitable policing styles and oppressive tendencies often exhibited by many rank and file officers in the discharge of their challenging task of security management have also not helped the matter.

Therefore, the prevailing public view is that the police are more likely to harass and extort from you rather than help you. As a result, majority of Nigerians do not see it as their duty to cooperate with the police or support its crime fighting duties.

The public perception is that the Police are biased in favour of the rich against the poor and government against the citizens. When a matter involves the rich and the poor, investigation is usually perceived (and there

---

[5] ibid

is some truth to this) as tilted in favour of the rich, so we have a situation where the average Nigerian does not find solace in the Police any longer.

There are many historical factors (as noted previously) that has led to the current unsatisfactory state of Nigerian police. The Nigerian police like others in post-colonial African nations is a creation of the colonial legacy and was set up as a tool of repression in the exercise of colonial hegemony over local communities.

For a long time in Nigeria, the police had been a tool of the state (this is still largely the case), mistrusted and feared by the people instead of being friend to the general public. As such, the public at large still see the police as an instrument of the ruling class that are always ready to unleash terror at the slightest opportunity.

This fact was emphasised by Robert Reiner when he stated that the police are the specialist carriers of the state's bedrock power: the monopoly of legitimate use of force. How and for what this is used speaks to the very heart of the condition of a political order. The danger of abuse, on behalf of particular partisan interests or the police themselves are clear and daunting.[6]

Constitutionally, the primary function of the Police is the maintenance of public order through crime detection and prevention so as to safeguard the lives of citizens and their property. It was for this reason that the phrase "the Police is your friend" is universally acceptable.

The duties and powers of the police are well articulated in the Police Act, 1943. Section 4 of the Act itemised the basic duties of the police as directly quoted below:

- prevention and detection of crime
- apprehension of offenders

---

[6] Robert Reiner (1993) "Police Accountability: Principles, Patterns and Practices" in R. Reiner and S. Spencer (eds.) *Accountability Policing: Effectiveness, Empowerment and Equity* (London: Institute of public Policy Research).

- preservation of law and order

- due enforcement of all laws and regulations with which they are directly, charged, and

- The performance of such other military duties within or outside Nigeria as may be required of them by or under the authority of the Act or any other Act.[7]

So the police in Nigeria are empowered by law to carry out global standard policing duties and enforcement of the law and keeping of the peace. These are typical idealistic roles and duties of the police in any democratic society.

This idealistic vision of the police roles was further explained by John Alderson's advocacy that the police should:

"contribute towards liberty, equality and fraternity ... help reconcile

---

[7] The Police Act 1943

freedom with security and to uphold the rule of law...facilitate human dignity though upholding and protecting human rights and pursuit of happiness...provide leadership and participation in dispelling crimogenic social conditions... contribute towards the creation and reinforcement of trust in communities, strengthen the security of persons and property and the feeling of security of persons, investigate, detect and activate the prosecution of offences, within the rule of law, curb public disorder, deal with major and minor cases and to help and advice those in distress where necessary".[8]

The absence of this idealistic advocacy ethos in their daily dealings with the police, has strengthened the public's view that the police are pro-politicians in power and anti the common citizen.

---

[8] Alemika EEO. Chukwuma I. Police community violence in Nigeria. Lagos, Centre for Law Enforcement Education and Human Rights Commission; 2000.

So, despite the legal powers granted to the police as highlighted above; most Nigerians do not agree that the police are doing a good job when it comes to crime prevention and public safety.

Consequently, Odinkalu stated that the *"police institution in Nigeria still have a long way to go in meeting its expectations especially in the areas of crime prevention and detection. The police are often not polite to victims of crime, because they are treated as mere sources of crime evidence and not as human beings."*[9]

With the absence of effective strategy to deliver Intelligence Led Policing for instance, the Nigerian police are mainly reactive in their work and this is inefficient as they seem to only show up after a crime as already been committed.

Intelligence Led Policing (ILP) aids law

---

[9] Odinkalu CA. When did police become your friend? Changing roles of civil society in promoting security and safety in Nigeria. In: Alemika EEO, Chukwuma IC. editor. Crime and policing in Nigeria: Challenges and option. Ikeja: Cleen Foundation; 2004.

enforcement in identifying, examining, and formulating preventative, protective, and responsive operations to specific targets, threats, and problems.

It is important to note that ILP is not a new policing model; rather, it is an integrated enhancement (and deliberate Join-up of isolated existing tools) that can contribute to public safety.

The dominant source of intelligence is the people. If the people are against the police; it will be impossible to build a credible intelligence picture to aid crime prevention and prosecution.

The police cannot be everywhere. Hence, the cooperation of the public is essential to support the police in successful crime prevention and prosecution.

This outcome cannot be achieved as long as the citizenry view the police with suspicion and fear. So, improving the perception of the police and enhancing support for them is essential to its ability to deliver its constitutional duties and ensure civil security of the nation.

The public's perceptions of how police treat them appear to affect their willingness to obey the law and obey the police. So a more positive image and perception of the police will lead to better obedience of the law by the people.

CATEGORIES OF PUBLIC POLICE PERCEPTIONS

Through research, I have found that the established trio of factors (Mastrofski,1998) that shapes public perception of the police applies totally in Nigeria.

These are:

- General perceptions of the police as an **organisation** or institution.

- Perceptions of police **outcomes**, and

- Perceptions of police **processes**.

General perceptions of the police as an organisation or institution.
The general image of the police offers an overview of the public's perception of the police as an organisation. The perception of the people of the police as an institution is not always based on individual personal experience or interaction with the police.

The following are examples of overall perception factors:
- ➢ Confidence in the police
- ➢ Satisfaction with the police
- ➢ Trust in the police
- ➢ Respect for the police
- ➢ Support for the police
- ➢ Police performance in general

The benefit of such general descriptions is that they reflect an overall orientation of the public to the police.

They give us a general sense of how positive or negative the public is toward the police. They are limited, however, in that they provide no indication of what it is about the police that pleases or displeases them.

Truth is, the vast majority of Nigerians rarely have direct personal contact with the police in their day to day life. Hence, these general perceptions can easily be shaped by media reports, rumours, family and friends' prejudices and hearsay, established myths as well as observed activities of the police.

Police organisation through their various public relations officers, reel out policies to try and reassure the public of change but people do not buy this as actions speak louder than words. Simply stated, it is not what you say to the public about how good you are at policing that convinces them.

It is what the public feels about the police based upon what they see and experience every day that matters. Whether we want to acknowledge this or not, perception is reality to the public.

The more citizens perceive the police to be honest and caring about their interests, the more they will comply with police directives and decisions. In a report on corruption index in 2017, the Nigerian National Bureau of Statistics put the police as the most corrupt agency of government at 46.4%.[10]

The police protested this finding but most observers believe the police had no choice but to protest otherwise that will be tantamount to accepting they are corrupt. Other government agencies were also indicted with the Immigration service at 30.7%, Tax/Revenue Agencies at 27.3%, Customs at 26.5% and the driving Licensing Agency at 28.5%.

There is therefore widespread unanimity that the majority of Nigerians perceive the police as corrupt; thus starving the police of the goodwill and cooperation they should be enjoying from the public.

HOW IS THE POLICE PERCEIVED BY THE PUBLIC IN NIGERIA?11

---

[10] http://www.nigerianstat.gov.ng/. Accessed on 29 August 2017
[11] This is based on our own research findings

1) Do you trust the Police: *94% said NO*

2) Do you think the Police are doing a good Job in relation to Crime & Disorder: *90% said NO*

3) Will you report a crime you witness to the police: *95% said NO*

4) Will you report a crime you are a victim of to the Police : *80% said NO*

5) Do you think the Police act ethically with the public: *80% said NO*

6) Do you think the Police are well paid and looked after by Government*: 60% said NO*

7) Do you think majority of the Police are corrupt: *98% of People said YES*

8) Do you think majority of the Police are Corrupt: *70% of Police Officers said YES*

It is therefore fair to say, majority of Nigerians do not trust the police, hence the perception of the police as an organization is largely negative. Any attempt to improve the image and perception of the police will need to address this fundamental issue of public mistrust in the institution.

Similar research was conducted by Oxford University on the public perception of the police in Nigeria few years ago. Some of their key conclusions which supports our own findings are as follows:[12]

   i.   Nearly one-half (48.5%) of the respondents felt somewhat or very unsafe in meeting the police.

   ii.   Only 6.3% of the respondents felt that the police were effective most of the time in preventing or containing violent conflicts.

   iii.   Only 6.4% of those interviewed expressed a lot of trust in the police; an additional 16.7% said they somewhat trust the police.

In their policy conclusion, the Oxford Briefing Paper declared as follows:

---

[12] Improving Institutions for Pro-Poor Growth (iiG). Briefing Paper. CSAE Economics Dept· University of Oxford

"Our research reveals a general lack of confidence in the capacity of the police to prevent and contain insecurity in Nigeria. Citizens lack trust in the police and there is a need to strengthen policy to enhance the capability of the police for effective service delivery, and to enhance public confidence in the law enforcement agency."[13]

The Oxford findings clearly point to the need to develop the capability and trustworthiness of the Nigerian police so that the law enforcement agency can serve as an effective public agency for the preservation of safety and order in the country.[14]

So the social environment has a pervasive influence on public perception. People's attitude is influenced by the opinions prevailing in the social group to which they belong.

---

[13] ibid
[14] ibid

In short, the person's family friends, community, place of work, school or club can influence public perception. The perception of police as an institution can be a big product of dominant and persistent media depictions of it.

Perceptions of police outcomes.
Outcomes are identified by knowing the goals that people hold for the police. The constitutional mandate gives the police a massive range of powers to maintain civil security and community cohesion.

Despite its wide-ranging powers, most of the public perception of police outcomes is focused on the impact the police have on crime and public safety. Confidence in the ability of the police to achieve traditional crime-focused goals appears to be very low indeed.

Only ten percent of respondents have a good perception of the police in relation to crime focused outcomes.

Unlike the general perception of the police as an institution; perception of police outcomes tends to be based on more detailed knowledge or experience of the works of the police.

The expectations of the citizens on the ability of the police to achieve crime prevention or criminal apprehension has been decimated over the years with the inability of the police to resolve high profile crimes.

A few years ago, the Attorney General of the country was murdered by gunmen in his own home,[15] despite police security attachments to him.

Nobody was ever charged for that criminal act. Many other high-profile politicians have been killed and also no arrest or conviction has taken place.

So, the thinking is that if an Attorney General can be killed with the police being unable to

---

[15]   https://www.vanguardngr.com/2016/07/buhari-orders-igp-re-open-bola-ige-dokubos-cases/. Accessed on 20 August 2017

make any arrest; then mere citizens definitely have no hope.

There are those who may have some little confidence in the police as an institution but not in their ability to achieve crime related outcomes.

Perceptions of police processes.
The processes of policing are how police do their work. The aspects of police processes that one might study are virtually infinite, but the public cares most about those that are captured by the notion of "service."

Service has many dimensions, some of which are generalizable to a wide variety of human services and not just policing: attentiveness, reliability, responsiveness, competence, manners, fairness, and integrity.

Some features of service are peculiar to police – those aspects of their authority that empower them to intrude on citizens' privacy and coerce them: interrogation techniques, stop and search and use of force, for example.

There are distinct emotions attached to perceptions of police process delivery because it tends to be based on personalised experiences of respondents and their dealings with the police.

For instance, 95% of respondents believe the police are motivated by corruption and bribe taking when they stop drivers at check points. So, the process of stopping and checking at check points is not seen as legitimate police work but financially motivated exercises.

A study in England found that citizens were more likely to feel fairly treated when officers gave a good reason for the stop. But this is not the practice in Nigeria.

The public image of the honesty and ethical standards of police officers for instance is very low. Only 20% of respondents felt the police work to any ethical standard whatsoever.

Internationally, a growing body of research suggests that how the public feels about the way police treat them affects the public's behaviour (obeying the law and obeying the police). Most of this research is based on studies of citizen contacts with the police.

So, from our own research findings, the referenced study from Oxford University and also the corruption index report by the Nigerian National Bureau of Statistics (a government agency); there is an issue of corruption and lack of public trust in the police.

This is a major cause of the mistrust of the police by Nigerians. I will try to proffer some solutions to this in later Chapters of this book.

WISDOM OF A SAGE

"The test of police efficiency is the ABSENCE of crime and disorder, not the VISIBLE evidence of police action in dealing with it."

— Sir Robert Peel

CHAPTER TWO

COMMUNITY POLICING AS A TOOL FOR COMMUNITY SUPPORT

The concept of community policing is premised on the fact that most people are law abiding. It is a form of "Normative Sponsorship Theory" proposition. This assumes that most people are citizens of good will and that they will cooperate with others to build consensus as long as they have shared common values.

It is not my intention in this Chapter to fully discuss community policing in great details; that will distract from the focus of this book. But I want to discuss this subject as a way of illustrating the necessity of community engagement and buy-in.

Community consent is essential for peaceful policing. For example, the reason why we stop at traffic lights may have little to do with the law and more to do with creating a safe environment for ourselves and those we care about.

So, in order to protect ourselves and loved ones; we will do what we think will help to achieve that outcome. Hence cooperating with the police will become instinctive as long as people buy into how the police work and are recognised as essential stakeholders.

The community-policing philosophy rests on the belief that law-abiding citizens in the community have a responsibility to participate in the police process. It also rests on the belief that solutions to today's contemporary community problems demand freeing both community residents and law enforcement to explore creative ways to address neighbourhood concerns beyond a narrow focus on individual crimes.

In April 2004, President Obasanjo introduced a community policing programme for the Nigeria Police at a launch in Enugu. Some pilot was supposed to followed in designated communities. But as with everything else in Nigeria, nothing more was heard about it again.

Then in September 2017, the current IGP (IGP Idris) re-launched the initiative again, complete with a new logo. He also established a Community Policing Management Committee to move things forward. In my view, this is still largely a top down approach which may not deliver as expected.

Community policing is a proactive approach to preventing crime. It allows for law enforcement to
   • Examine crime trends

- Analyse and work toward positive alternatives to community and neighbourhood conditions

- Educate and involve communities in crime prevention strategies

- Create an atmosphere of zero tolerance toward crime and criminal activity

Some examples of proactive policing are:
- Helping the community start community watch programs
- Conducting security surveys for homes and communities
- Encouraging people to engrave their properties with personal identifiers
- Encouraging people to register equipment and maintain logs of all their valuables
- Having high-quality locks and lighting on personal property and within Communities.

EMBRACING COMMUNITY POLICING CONCEPTS

Community policing is a philosophy that promotes and supports organizational strategies to address the causes of crime, to reduce the fear of crime and social disorder through problem-solving tactics and community-police partnerships.[16]

Also, according to the US Department of Justice: "Community policing is a philosophy that promotes organizational strategies, which support the systematic use of partnerships and problem-solving techniques, to proactively address the immediate conditions that give rise to public safety issues such as crime, social disorder and fear of crime."[17]

Worldwide experiments with community policing since the 1970s are widely regarded as having contributed to a welcome progress of law enforcement organizations. After years of organizational distance from their

---

[16] Source: Community Oriented Policing Services Office, USA
[17] http://www.cops.usdoj.gov/default.asp?item=36

communities, the police are taking stock of their position in society and in relation to citizens.

Strong police-public relationships make for mutual respect, confidence, and improved information flow. Community policing also has significant potential for handling the challenges presented by the changing nature of crime.

Crime can no longer be thought of only in terms of isolated incidents of victimization. Crime has come to represent a series of phenomena, from low level anti-social behaviour, youth delinquency, urban poverty and addiction induced criminality to stalking, domestic abuse to hate crimes and serious offences. So knowing and cooperating with the community is essential to successful policing in the 21st century.

Crime is intra-community and requires local solutions; these facts make a case for attentive policing that is sensitive to the dynamics within different states, cities, neighbourhoods and groups and is geared to community safety.

In developed countries, the police are seen as needing to work with communities, sharing responsibility and being creative in applying joint resources to recurring problems and to advancing community well-being.

So the lack of community support of the police in Nigeria is a major hindrance to effective policing. This chasm between the police and most Nigerian communities has become larger over the last twenty years. With many communities employing private security and local militias to protect themselves, the relevance of the official police as a community asset has been lost. There are communities all over Nigeria that do not see the police for years and years.

The police in Nigeria are not known for their preventive and proactive posture. They tend to show up only after crime has been committed. When last did you hear of a police intelligence operation infiltrating criminal gangs and preventing criminality in Nigeria? That hardly ever happens.

In fact; 80% of our respondents said they will not report a crime of which they are victims to the police, unless very serious crime that caused injury or death occurs. Chief among the reasons given was the lack of trust in police outcomes and processes.

While having agreed universal principles, in practice, community policing could mean different things to different people. This is not an easy concept to successfully implement anywhere in the world. But the backdrop of public mistrust makes the Nigerian case even more challenging. The nature of community policing remains ambiguous from nation to nation.

It is not clear, for example, whether community policing is a means to an end or an end in itself. Though police-community partnerships, problem solving, and crime reduction efforts in communities are widely recognized characteristics, there is arguably no consensus on the overall mission of community policing.

Its ethos emphasizes the importance of local delivery, yet for what overall purpose? Is community policing primarily about effective crime control by the police, supported by partnership work with communities?

Is the goal about building community trust and confidence in the professional police? Or, is the goal to strengthen communities to create natural resistance to crime, promoting self-policing by communities? Is community policing more about reforming professional policing or changing the role of the public?

The leadership team of the Nigeria Police therefore need to decide what its community policing agenda and purposes are. Activities can then be designed to deliver the prescribed outcomes.

Extra financial provisions will need to be found to deliver community policing as it is not a cheap proposition to deliver. It is labour intensive as more officers are needed to be visible in the communities.

But the current numerical strength of the Nigerian police is tolerable to begin implementation of community policing with some policy changes put in place.

The Nigerian police simply need to become more proactive and focused on crime prevention rather than simply responding to crimes after it has taken place.

Community policing also needs to be implemented together with Intelligence Led Policing. I have written a book[18] on how Intelligence Led Policing can be delivered in Nigeria; so I will not repeat the strategies here.

Engagement with the community will yield a treasure trove of intelligence that will feed into an Intelligence Led Policing operational strategy in the country.

---

[18] Omole C. *Implementing Intelligence-Led Policing in Nigeria.* 20117

LESSONS FROM HISTORY

Sir Peel was a British MP. It was during his term in Parliament that Peel acknowledged the rising crime statistics and sought to improve the methods of crime prevention. As a result, in 1829, he brought about the Metropolitan Police Act and the first disciplined police force in greater London.

Before this, as Home Secretary in 1822, Peel introduced the Constabulary Act, and the Constabulary Police of Ireland was formed. Both of these police forces, still exist till today. As a pioneer in police administration globally, Peel produced some essential principles that should guide policing.

Sir Robert Peel's Nine Principles of Policing[19]

1. The basic mission of the police is to prevent crime and disorder.

---

[19] These are well recorded principles by Peel that is noted in several publications too many to reference

2. The ability of the police to perform their duties is dependent upon public approval of police actions.

3. Police must secure the willing cooperation of the public, in voluntary observance of the law to be able to secure and maintain the respect of the public.

4. The degree of cooperation of the public that can be secured diminishes proportionally to the necessity of the use of force.

5. Police seek and preserve public favour, not by catering to public opinion but by constantly demonstrating absolute impartial service to the law.

6. Police use physical force to the extent necessary to secure observance of the law or to restore order only when the expertise of persuasion, advice, and warning is found to be insufficient.

7. Police at all times should maintain a relationship with the public, that gives

reality to the historic tradition; the police are public and the public are the police. The police being the only full-time individuals charged with the duties that are incumbent on all of the citizens.

8. Police should always direct their actions strictly toward their functions and never appear to usurp the powers of the judiciary.

9. The test of police efficiency is the absence of crime and disorder not the visible evidence of police action in dealing with it.

The main thrust of these principles conceives the police more as a service to the community and working in partnership with it rather than a paramilitary organization meant to oppress the people.

The community focused history of policing in Western democracies is in distinct contrast with the African colonial oppressive purpose of policing in the past century.

FUNDAMENTAL PRINCIPLES OF COMMUNITY POLICING.[20]

The central premise of community policing is that the level of **community participation** in enhancing safety and social order and in solving community related crime should be raised since the police cannot carry out this task on their own.[21]

In order to achieve such partnerships, the police must be **better integrated into the community** and strengthen their legitimacy through policing by consent and improving their services to the public.

They should therefore:

- ➢ be visible and accessible to the public;
- ➢ know and be known by, the public;
- ➢ respond to the communities' needs;
- ➢ listen to the communities' concerns;
- ➢ engage and mobilise the communities;

---

[20] As contained in a report titled: Good Practices in Building Police-Public Partnerships by the Senior Police Adviser to the OSCE Secretary General. 2008
[21] ibid

> ➢ be accountable for their activities and the outcome of these activities.[22]

Based on global best practice; key strategies for the translation of these principles into practice include:

> ➢ creating fixed geographic neighbourhood areas with permanently assigned police officers;
> ➢ introducing visible and easily accessible police officers and police facilities;
> ➢ reorienting patrol activities to emphasize non-emergency servicing;
> ➢ engaging communities;
> ➢ introducing a pro-active problem-solving approach;
> ➢ involving all government agencies and services;
> ➢ involving all branches of the police.[23]

When members of a community are involved with each other, they know

> ➢ Their neighbours

---

[22] ibid
[23] ibid

> ➤ The daily "goings-on" in the neighbourhood
> ➤ When something is wrong.

Invariably, community policing is a philosophy, not a program. Hence it can be implemented in diverse forms as long as the basic ethos of the philosophy is understood and reflected.

This Chapter is not meant to be an exhaustive discussion on community policing; but a snapshot of the concept to enable a better understanding of the dynamics and dimensions of Police-Public relationship in Nigeria.

A more detailed analysis of community policing will have to include discussions about community justice, restorative justice and problem-oriented policing. That will be subjects of another book in future focusing on how community policing can be implemented in Nigeria.

This book is about the overarching subject of improving relationship between the community and the police. Starting with small changes, as suggested in the final Chapter of this book, can make an enormous difference in how the police think, speak, practice, and promote the meaning of community policing.

WISDOM OF A SAGE

Law enforcement officers are never 'off duty.'
They are dedicated public servants who are
sworn to protect public safety at any time and
place that the peace is threatened. They need all
the HELP THAT THEY CAN GET.

- Barbara Boxer

CHAPTER THREE

FACTORS INFLUENCING POLICE-COMMUNITY RELATIONS

There are several factors that influences the perception of the police by the public. But we will focus only on the salient factors in this chapter.

There appear to be at least three ways in which the public forms negative impressions of police: the direct experiences of the public with the police, how the police are presented to the public through the press and entertainment media, and the standards and expectations the public holds for the police.

DIRECT EXPERIENCES OF THE PUBLIC

Whilst the majority of Nigerians have not had a personal one to one encounter with the police; those that have rarely have any positive thing to say about the police.

In our research, it is hard to find a Nigerian that has a positive testimony of personal experience with the police. Many that admitted they have had some positive encounters said they have equally had much more negative encounters as well that their overall verdict become a negative one.

Testimony of consistently positive encounters (at least for majority of encounters) with the police was impossible to find in our research.

The depictions of police activities by the entertainment world and Nollywood helps to reinforce many of the negative perception further by focus on bad conducts, corruption and brutalization by the the police on the public.

Our research shows that for every one person extorted or brutalized by the police, twenty others will be negatively influenced by that one person.

So if only 5Million Nigerians have had a one to one encounter with the police in the past, 100Million Nigerians will be influenced by the testimonies (both real and exaggerated) of the 5Million.

This is how the majority of Nigerians have developed a negative image of the police even though when asked many could not recollect a personal experience of their own. A lot is based on feedback and media influences. This exponential contagion effect is what the police do not understand.

Behaving badly or mistreating one Nigerian can negatively shape the perception of twenty others (who may never encounter the police themselves). This is indeed food for thought for the rank and file officers.

HOW THE POLICE ARE PRESENTED TO THE PUBLIC THROUGH THE PRESS

The media are powerful players in shaping public opinion in Nigeria. Given the high level of illiteracy in the country, many wrongly assumes that as long as an item is in the news it must be correct.

Capacity for critical thinking and questioning of facts is not common place in Nigeria. So a repeated line of story about the police will create believability in many people, thus influencing perception of the police as an institution.

In a seminal work on the image of the police commissioned in 2001,[24] it was established that there are three theoretical approaches for explaining mass media effects on public attitudes about institutions such as the police (Fox and Van Sickel, 2001:6-8). These three approaches were explained in the report as follows:

---

[24] The Final Report to The International Association of Chiefs of Police by The Administration of Justice Program George Mason University in 2001

The "hypodermic needle" theory assumes that the public takes in media presentations like a drug, which produces powerful and long-term effects on their views of institutions such as the police. Members of the public are viewed as independent consumers of these media presentations, which they use to answer questions about the police and from which they formulate attitudes and perceptions of the police.[25]

The "limited effects" theory also assumes that the public uses the media for information, but it argues that individuals evaluate that information in the context of what they know from other sources – such as direct contact, family, friends, etc.[26]

These pre-existing and more-or-less independent impressions are believed to constitute powerful influences with which

---

[25] ibid
[26] ibid

media images must contend in the competition for influencing the public's views of the police. Under these circumstances, the effects of the mass media are expected to be present, but limited.[27]

The "subtle/minimal effects" theory falls in between the "hypodermic needle" and "subtle/minimal effects" theories.

Here, the hypothesized media effects are neither overwhelming nor minimal, but rather work in special ways by:
a) agenda setting – instructing the public in what to think about as the most important issues (e.g., whether policing is an important issue at a given time and what aspects are important).

b) priming – associating people or institutions with particular issues (e.g., associating the police with crime fighting).

---

[27] ibid

c) framing – shaping how to think about a given issue by either identifying general trends or covering specific events (e.g., how often the police use excessive force in dealing with suspects).[28]

Thus, all three theories posit that the mass media influence the public's views, although in different ways and to different degrees.[29]

The influence of media coverage is substantial in shaping perception of the police. And from all intent and purposes, it seems the police are losing the media war.

The mass media tend to concentrate on the "sensationalistic, personal, lurid, and tawdry details of unusual and high-profile police activities and failures. This has not been helpful. The police therefore just respond to stories rather than shape them.

---

[28] ibid
[29] ibid

UNFAIR MEDIA COVERAGE

There is power in persistent negative portrayal. In this regard, the media in general have not be fair to the Nigerian police. The Media (especially the social media) is full of negative depiction and stories about the police.

Some are rightfully deserved but plenty are untrue and manufactured stories or stories intended to drive an agenda. But when the expectation of the citizenry is so low, they will believe anything negative that is written about the police.

All the outstanding work being done by many police officers is rarely covered by the media. But the biggest challenge here is the failure of the police organisation to shape the news proactively in a proactive way. Like its policing approach it is overwhelmingly reaction and after the fact response.

The Nigerian police do not know how to sell itself. And there is absence of a coherent media and communication strategy. In short public perception is shaped by what is told to the public. Regarding the police; who is doing the telling? Definitely not the police.

The media landscape in Nigeria is in free fall in my opinion. No effective statutory or self-regulation is in place and it is full of biased reporting, propaganda, politically motivated reporting, incompetence and pervasive corruption. Yes corruption.

The media both online and traditional outfits give prominence to stories that should never even make the inside pages, spin stories beyond recognition and many journalists are lazy and will only report legitimate stories if financially induced to do so.

Don't get me wrong, there are some outstanding journalists in Nigeria, but the professional practitioners who work to proper ethical code are few indeed and many try to keep their heads down so as not to attract the wrath of their militant colleagues. So this is not an indictment on all the media in Nigeria. I know some fantastic journalists in Nigeria.

With most media organisations in Nigeria owned by politicians or their surrogates, it is no surprise that the landscape is as polluted as it is. So there has to be big health warnings to stories coming out of the traditional media.

The online organised media are a bit better but they also have their problems. The bigger challenges with the online media is the problem of Citizens Journalism (CJ).

This is where individuals on social media report whatever they like and say whatever they want without any sense of responsibility.

There have been many trending stories sourced from these mischief makers with many people misled and misinformed. So the media management of the police need to be more robust and proactive.

Accordingly, the focus of the police mainly on the traditional media outfits (whose influence are diminishing in Nigeria urban landscape) is also a failed strategy.

At the same time, there is little or no social media strategy for the police in Nigeria. In fact, they are nearly non-existent as an organization in the social media space. But I will be addressing this more in the next Chapter.

THE STANDARDS AND EXPECTATIONS THE PUBLIC HOLDS FOR THE POLICE

Due to the historical negative opinions of the police by the public, the expectation of the police by Nigerians is very low.

With many paying for personal security in their streets and estates, the expectation of police outcome and deliverables is at rock bottom.

For many, the police have become a last resort rather than a first call. It is difficult to have affection for an institution you see as unproductive and unsupportive of your life.

The only silver lining in this scenario is that many Nigerians are frustrated with Nigerian government institutions as a whole of which the police may be a prominent example. So this is not a unique frustration and despair for Nigerians.

But for those still optimistic about the emergence of a new Nigeria in the future, there is an expectation that the police will be reformed and transformed as the nation changes to become the Nigeria of our dream.

OTHER FACTORS SHAPING PUBLIC PERCEPTION
In addition to the key influencers discussed above, there are a few other perception-shapers of the public. These are:

Crime Rate or Perception of it
Public perception of the level of crime and disorder in their neighbourhood and

community is a significant factor shaping their opinion of the police.

When each day starts with news of kidnappings, armed robberies, murders and so on; it is hard to think positively about the police (who are supposed to be fighting crimes). Each of these news represents a failure of policing. So the police will be negatively perceived with increasing crime and criminality.

The Media
While the media is a general influencer of public perception of the police; research shows that a change of media focus can change many minds.

This is because the perceptions that are most difficult to change are those formed as a result of encounters with the police rather those formed by media biases and propaganda. As previously discussed, the media exerts influence on public opinion in a significant way.

The negative perception increases even more during major media coverage of police excesses.

Contact with the Police
This is the strongest perception shaper. And people who develop a negative perception of the police through personal encounters tend to have the strongest negative position that is difficult to shift even by a positive media campaign subsequently.

Officer Demeanour and Approach.
The measure of officer demeanour was formed from some questions that asked respondents whether police were respectful, trustworthy, fair, or helpful and how concerned they acted. Over 70% said the demeanour of police officers they have seen was intimidating and unhelpful.

This contributes to the negative perception of the police and it reinforces a lot of the adverse media coverage and depictions of police officers. Sadly, the police more often act to support the negative caricature created by the media of them rather than dispel it. Respect is reciprocal. Showing respect to the public will more often than not create a respectful response back. But the angry and unfriendly look of many officers puts the public on the edge and on the defensive almost immediately contact is made.

Prior Victimisation
Prior victimization, especially violent crime victimization, significantly lowers peoples' approval of the police. Feeling that the police were not there when they were needed reduces affection for them.

So with the increasing rate of criminality in Nigeria, partly due to the difficult economic conditions, creates more victims of crime who in turn develop a dislike for the police who are seen as ineffective.

Knowledge
The Nigerian police are massively misunderstood by Nigerians. Many do not know the huge obstacles and constraints the

police face day to day. From poor funding, outdated equipment and low motivation of the rank and file, the police are trying against all the odds against them.

It seems the more knowledgeable a person is of the full challenges facing the police, the better sympathy they develop for them. But the Nigeria Police is a highly insular and relatively secretive organisation.

This makes access to this detailed knowledge difficult and only the select few know about these problems confronting the police. It is the duty of the police to make itself understood and more effort is needed in openness and candid public engagement.

Politics and Government
The more negatively the public perceive the government of the day, the more badly they tend to see the police.

As the law enforcement tool of the government, the police can be vicariously blamed for the failings of the government as a visible and easily accessible face of the government.

A more positively disposed population to the government tend to see the police in better light too.

Economic Status
Our research found that the richer a person is; the better perception of the police they usually have. Drilled down further, it was found that this is due to the fact that rich people can pretty much get what they want from the police.

The police also respond better and more efficiently to wealthy people than they do to the poor. Many believe this is largely influenced by expectation of the reward and compensation provided by the rich. This is a dimension of the corruption that the public want eradicated.

Lack of Professional Pride
From time to time, there are scandals in the media about wealthy and influential people

in society corruptly using their influence to get their children jobs at major federal institutions. From the Central Bank of Nigeria to key federal ministries and other top agencies.

But it has never been reported that they do the same for the police. In fact, these wealthy families make sure their children do not join the police. So many Nigerians see the police as a basket case populated mainly by the worst of society. This of course is not true.

But the absence of the children of the rich and famous in the police tend to affirm the believe of many that the police is so bad and polluted, even the rich do not want their children to be tainted by it.

How else can you explain a family expending all their goodwill and influence to get their son a job with the Central Bank but will not even contemplate doing same for a job in the police.

In our research, 60% of respondents stated that they will see the police in better light if children of the rich and famous are joining and visibly represented.

Excessive Use of Force
There is nothing that gets an average Nigerian angry when asked about the police like the subject of the excessive use of force by the officers on the public. The police are seen as harassing with impunity and their penchant for the use of force (sometimes deadly force) on unarmed citizens is a major source of negative perception as well as deterrence against engagement with the police; even as a victim of crime.

WISDOM OF A SAGE

_____

Let's talk about policing and public safety. Let's

debate what works and what does not. We

must ABANDON PRACTICES THAT DO NOT

WORK, and do more of the things that actually

do work to save lives.

- Martin O'Malley

_____

CHAPTER FOUR

IMPROVING MEDIA ENGAGEMENT AND SOCIAL MEDIA EXPLOITATION

The Nigerian police as an institution is not effective in the use of the media to promote its image. This applies to both traditional media and social media. Although their use of the social media is significantly much worse.

The police seem to focus all its engagement on the traditional media, although the media landscape in Nigeria has changed significantly over the past twenty years.

The monopoly of the traditional media has been broken with the advent of social media. More Nigerians now access their news from the internet and social media than through traditional print and broadcast media.

The use of the internet and social media by the police is shockingly poor and uncoordinated in Nigeria. Developing ability to communicate with the public much faster is one of the current methods used by law enforcement agencies to protect the public, according to Hanson (2011). The evolvement of law enforcement tools were from "wanted posters" to "police radio (Hanson, 2011)."[30] And now the effective tools are social networks.

SOCIAL MEDIA ENGAGEMENT AND USAGE IN NIGERIA

Sixteen million Nigerians visit Facebook monthly. Nigeria already has one of the

---

[30] Hanson, W. (2011). How social media is changing law enforcement. *Government technology.* Accessed from http://www.govtech.com/public-safety/How-Social-Media-Is-Changing-Law-Enforcement.html

continent's highest smartphone penetration rates and that number will get even higher as smartphone subscriptions are expected to reach 95 million by 2019.[31]

Facebook said it has 7.2 million daily users from Nigeria with 97% of them accessing the platform via mobile. The use of traditional media has diminished by 50% in ten years in our urban areas. This is due to power problems for broadcast media and increased cost of newspapers.[32]

BEST PRACTICES IN POLICE SOCIAL MEDIA ADAPTATION
To succeed in the internet age, the police need to embrace more openly the use of the social media in furtherance of their duties.

To examine this subject, we will be looking at it from the following perspectives:

1) Social Media as a Source of Criminal

---

[31] https://qz.com/611516/more-people-use-facebook-in-nigeria-than-anywhere-else-in-africa/
[32] ibid

Information

2) Having a Voice in Social Media

3) Social Media to Push Information

4) Social Media to Leverage the Wisdom of the Crowd

5) Social Media to Interact with the Public

6) Social Media for Community Policing

7) Social Media to Show the Human Side of Policing

8) Social Media to Support Police IT Infrastructure

9) Social Media for Efficient Policing

Social Media as a Source of Criminal Information
The vanity in our culture makes the social media a rich source of intelligence for certain kinds of criminality, since we like to show off.

A lot of crimes have now moved online...and the Police need to become up to date with skills and competency to get ahead of the criminals.

Even terrorists prefer social media to normal email as it is a bigger haystack from which a needle will be more difficult to find they believe.

The police need to establish links with social media companies through International partners to allow access into data. As a minimum the police need to become very active on social media to begin to exploit its potential.

Having a Voice on Social Media
While there are many different and specific ways of using social media for policing beyond an information source for investigations, they can be framed under the general concept of using social media as a communication tool with the public and thereby establishing a police presence and voice on social media.

While this concept is currently being used

only in selected forces in African countries, the largely favourable public response and positive results make it essential that police forces work on establishing their own voice on social media a common practice in itself.

Social Media to Push Information
As media consumption, especially with the younger generation, shifts from local newspapers, television and radio to social media, police forces face the challenge to disseminate information to these audiences and thus increasingly need to use social media if they want to communicate to certain citizen groups.

Here, social media provide the possibility for police forces to publish news on their own without the traditional press as an intermediate and push information to a large number of readers directly. Using social media, police forces can embed their information in the new media channels that citizens use frequently in their daily lives.

By using social media this way, police forces

become more independent from the traditional press and open an immediate unfiltered connection to the general public. Many public safety challenges like riots and protests have a large social media use for organising and propagating it.

Social Media to Leverage the Wisdom of the Crowd
Social media provides police forces the opportunity to get information from the general public.

When pushing information to selected audiences who can easily further share the messages with their individual groups, police forces are connected to large crowds of people who they can ask for information.

Identifying suspects or issuing search warrants on social media has been highly successful for police forces in Germany for example.

While publishing search warrants and asking the public for help is a common police practice, social media brings a powerful lever to this existing practice. Social media may revitalize the instrument of public support in police operations that is currently not effective.

For the Hannover police (Germany), a review of the current effectiveness of search warrants revealed that there is only very little response to search warrants posted in newspapers or in public places.

On the other hand, search initiatives promoted by citizens on social media have been shown to have wide impact whilst lacking the professional experience of the police.

These two reasons, specifically, have been the drivers of the Police forces starting their own Facebook presence, which they primarily set up and use to publish search warrants and request help with identification of suspects.

Even though the force only published a few

messages every month, they have passed 100,000 Facebook friends who commonly share the police messages with their friends. In the search warrants the police asks the people to use a regular police phone number to report information. So the Information flows back into traditional channel.

Social Media to Interact with the Public
For the police, social media has the option to engage in a two-way, interactive dialogue with citizens. Communication with the public allows the police to answer questions of an individual in a way that it becomes shared knowledge and is accessible for others, too.

Most forces enter social media by pushing messages in a similar way that they previously offered for press announcements. After using social media for longer periods, police forces tend to use social media in a more interactive way by directly and publicly engaging in dialogue with individual citizens.

This is a consequence of the ways social media is designed. Twitter, for instance, allows anybody to craft messages, which mention another Twitter user.

This user is then notified of that message and can choose to reply. In many cases this conversation, different from email, takes place publicly, so that anybody else may choose to read it, too.

Social Media for Community Policing
Community policing is a concept that suggests a close collaboration between the police, the general public, and other organizations to increase safety in society.

Policing, thus, is not a matter of the police alone but rather a joined effort of different public actors. Community policing requires officers on a local level to develop a personal and close connection to citizen groups.

Social media has been successfully used by a number of police forces around the world to support community policing. Additionally, police forces have extended their community policing efforts to online communities.

For community policing, social media can empower the local officer in doing his job. In particular, in the Netherlands and the United Kingdom; social media officers have been appointed, who are responsible for social media communication in their local communities, or social media has become a standard tool for a community police office.

Using all channels of communication to reach out to the community is essential to fostering better relations and understanding.

Social Media to Show the Human Side of Policing
When using social media, police forces need to choose the tone of their messages that they use to talk with the public.

Usually, police communication is characterized by a formal and impersonal tone. Typically, communication relates to facts from current operations made in official statements.

The experience of different police forces globally shows that social media not only calls for a different tone, it also allows police officers to talk about positive news, emotions, police culture and experiences of daily life.

As a result, the public describes and welcomes the police as a human organization that can be trusted.

Social Media to Support Police IT Infrastructure
In cases of large-scale crises or in cases of investigations that receive special attention by the public, police systems for communication with the public come under stress.

Increased attention and demand for the information of a selected force or command may exceed their geographic boundaries and can go way beyond the local community that the police force is usually responsible for, as local news can be virally distributed through social media.

Usually, the IT infrastructures behind Police websites and other channels are not able to cope with the peaks in demand.

One successful way of dealing with the high demands has been the use of various social media sites that can better balance high loads in their global infrastructures. This way the police can use the existing resilient infrastructure of social media firms as leverage to extend its reach.

Social Media for Efficient Policing
Currently, police forces across the globe are confronted with the task of performing their work with reduced financial resources, due to budget cuts following the economic downturn.

By using social media, many police forces have been able to increase the efficiency of their communication and develop a closer connection with the general public despite shrinking budgets.

The use of social media as a communication tool is an efficient means of policing. With the spread of Fake News, Citizens need to know how to get Authoritative News and Updates from the Police.

So the Nigerian police has a long way to go to leverage the social media as a tool for effective outreach to the community. I will be making recommendations about this in the final Chapter of the book.

The social media is an ungoverned space and millions of Nigerians have taken to these channels to vent their frustrations about the police.

The Internet is therefore full of true and untrue depictions of the police with no effective voice from the policing institution itself to counter many of these misrepresentations. The general attitude of the police institution towards the social media is that of non-engagement.

The Nigerian Police and Internet Utilisation

The police need to get the basics right before we can begin to talk about the big social media platforms. Take the Nigeria Police website as an example.

This is very badly put together and seems never updated operationally other than basic news postings. Outdated websites become abandoned portals that nobody want to visit. It also portrays the organisation as lethargic and old-school, unengaged with the modern world. Let me give you some examples.

During one of my sessions training senior officers of the Nigerian police in March 2017, I referred a senior police officer to the outdated information on the NPF website that stated that AIG Mbu is still in charge of Zone 2.

In reality, AIG Mbu left zone 2 in October 2015 and retired from the Force in 2016. As at 10th September 2017, the police website was still unchanged despite the officer assuring me he escalated the need for changes to the website to Force headquarters in March 2017 and I believe him.

So AIG Mbu who left zone 2 in October 2015 and retired from the police in 2016 is still showing as the officer in charge of zone 2 in September 2017 on the website managed by the headquarters of the Nigerian police. How bad can it get?
Similar changes have not been made to practically all the zones. The same NPF website is showing AIG Mohammed as being in charge of Zone 1. This again is two years out of date.

If the police are to gain credibility, the information contained on its portals have to be credible and authoritative. But it seems they are not getting the basics right. The following pages shows snapshots of the website captured in September 2017.

Information years out of date on the websites that it controls fully portend badly for their ability to maintain up to date information and status update on big social media platforms they do not control.

Getting the basics right is crucial for the police. The relationship with traditional media seem to be the overwhelming focus of the police leadership.

This is not only ineffective but also expensive and limiting. As a passionate friend of the police, it is my duty to say the truth in a constructive way to support the change and transformation we seek.

The slow pace of police responses to issues is at odds not only with the rapid 24hrs news cycle but only antithesis of the social media saturated world we live in.

The Nigeria Police need to become more agile and responsive. Police need to be leading the news and not being led by the news.

NIGERIA POLICE FORCE

Home   About Us ▾   Zone ▾   Departments ▾   Units ▾   Formation List ▾

Information ▾   Contact Us

ZONE 2

INTRODUCTION

Zone 2 Police Command located in the South-western geopolitical zone of Nigeria Comprises of Lagos and Ogun states. As at the time of collating this report, the zone was headed by AIG. Mbu Joseph Mbu. The entire zone has a Population of about 12,741,632 based on the 2006 population Census figures and combined police strength of 67,757 officers and men.

Lagos state according to the 2006 National population census figure has an estimated population of about 9,013,534 covering the 20 local government areas with a staff Strength of 29,122 Police Officers. Ogun state has an estimated population of 3,728,089. According to the 2006 Population census figure and staff strength of about 7,107 Police Officers.

In the year under review, Lagos State Police Command developed an intelligence driven crime combating Strategy under the mission Statement captioned "Zero level tolerance for crime", poised to rid the state of criminal elements and criminality and formulate strategies for better proactive & more effective policing. This strategy so formulated also measures the command's existing state of security and cushions the vehicular patrol system while also strengthens the pin-down points particularly of border towns to withstand the sophistication of criminal activities being perpetrated. In the same vein, information technology training programmes was put in place to enable officers and men meet up with the current trend in the world and bring crime to its barest minimum.

Police Website with outdated information captured on 10th September 2017.[33]

---

[33] http://npf.gov.ng/zone2.php

NIGERIA POLICE FORCE

Home   About Us ▾   Zone ▾   Departments ▾   Units ▾   Formation List ▾

Information ▾   Contact Us

ZONE 1

INTRODUCTION

Zone 1 Police command located in the North-Western Geo-political zone of Nigeria comprises of Jigawa, Kano and Katsina states. As at the time of compiling this report, the zone was headed by AIG Tambari Y. Mohammed, fwc. The entire zone covers an area of about 96,765 square kilometers with a population of about 19,254,909 based on the 2006 census figure and combined police strength of 18,358 Officers and men.

Katsina state according to the 2006 National population census figure has an estimated population of 5,792,578 covering the 34 Local Government Areas with staff strength of 4,143 Police officers.

Jigawa state has an estimated population of 4,348,649 based on the 2006 population census figure and combined staff strength of 5,281 Police officers. Kano state comprising of 44 Local Government Areas has a total land area of 38,650 square kilometers and a population of about 9,383,682 according to 2006 national census figure.

In the year under review, the Jigawa state police command recorded a total of 613 reported cases out of which, 309 were prosecuted, 207 were convicted, 14 were transferred and 83 were under investigation. 142 persons were arrested in connection with the reported cases. The value of properties lost stood at ₦809,700 while properties worth ₦551,865 were recovered.

Kano state command recorded a total of 530 cases out of which 108 were convicted, 1 was acquitted, 10 were closed, 26 were transferred, 61 were referred to Directorate of public prosecution, 84 were under investigation and 240 are awaiting trial. 4 assault rifles, 56 Improvised Explosive Device Materials, 2 AK 47 rifles, 2 pump action rifles, 1 Beretta pistol, 1 smoke gun and 433 live ammunitions were also recovered.

Katsina state command recorded a total of 509 cases out of which 394 were prosecuted, 110 were awaiting trial and 5 were under investigation. 814 persons were arrested in connection with the reported cases. Properties worth ₦10,474,969 were lost while properties worth ₦203,040 were recovered.

CONSTRAINTS

Police Website with outdated information captured on 10th September 2017[34]

---

[34] http://npf.gov.ng/zone1.php

NIGERIA POLICE FORCE

Home   About Us▾   Zone▾   Departments▾   Units▾   Formation List▾

Information▾   Contact Us

THE HISTORY OF NIGERIA POLICE FORCE

The word Police is derived from the Greek word "Polis", meaning that part of non-ecclesiastical administration having to do with the safety, health and order of the state. The Greek politeria, meant the art of governing and regulating the welfare, security needs and order of the city-state in the interest of the public.

Although Police is derived from the Greek, it was the Romans who perfected the system. The Roman politia meant the same thing as the Greek Politeira. It was a symbol of power residing in central Authority.

During the duration of the Roman Empire, Police in Rome was organized from the ranks. There was the Roman Prefect which had under his control fourteen Magistrates, each responsible for a district and assisted by vigiles who patrolled the streets, lictores who were law enforcement officers and stationaii who were residents of the city blocks.

In Britain, Policing developed as a local affair with a role which has remained till now. That it is the responsibility of every person to maintain law and order. This role is rooted in history and common law tradition of Britain that each citizen had a duty to suppress crime and disorder within his area. Failure to do so entailed the payment of fines

The burden of policing was placed on every adult citizen. It was an avocational obligatory policing, manifesting itself in the forms of tythingman of the Saxon Police, the frankpledge in the South and East of England after the Norman conquest 1066 and later as the Parish Constable system after the enactment of the Statute of Winchester 1285.

Before describing these systems in brief, it is relevant to observe that policing and police work did not start as a paid profession. It started as a noble, incorruptible profession with considerable responsibility and distinction. It was the Justices of the Peace system, which corrupted the Parish Constable System.

*This is the capture of the curious page on the Nigerian police website that is titled the **History of the Nigeria Police Force**. But the content is so unrelated.*

This "History of Nigeria Police Force" page started by stating as follows:

> "The word Police is derived from the Greek word "Polis", meaning that part of non-ecclesiastical administration having to do with the safety, health and order of the state. The Greek politeria, meant the art of governing and regulating the welfare, security needs and order of the city-state in the interest of the public".[35]

What on earth has the above introduction got to do with the history of our police? This is another example of how the police are not getting the basics right in terms of using the Internet to engage with the public, much less using social media platforms to drive its public relations.

This section on the police website ended by stating:

> "When the first paid professional police force was proposed in Britain,

---

[35] http://npf.gov.ng/History_Nigeria_Police.php. Accessed on 10th September 2017

it was strongly opposed by those who feared that such force would lead to repression and threat to the freedom of the individual and to democracy. The Police Force as we know it today went through three distinct stages before it became a profession. As Hewitt, W.A. puts it. "At first the populace, though small was responsible for maintaining law and order. Then Justices of the Peace emerged on the scene to provide both the law and order and Justice at the bar. Then, in the present era, paid professional police were established to maintain law and order."

There is nothing in this section about the history of the Nigerian police at all. Just some banal blurb that is completely unrelated and irrelevant. This is indeed an indictment of the public relations machinery of the police.

Police is a people business. So, it is time for police organizations to leverage social media to develop productivity of works, achieve organizational goals, and protect the public at the same time.

In my previous books, I have used the terms Nigeria Police Force to refer to the police. I am aware the Obasanjo regime amended the legislation that now refers to the police simply as "The Nigeria Police". But the police institution has not been consistent in using the new name as the word 'force' is currently present all over its website and other publications.

As you can see from the website capture in previous pages, the words 'Police Force' is still used on the police website. So I tried to use the familiar nomenclature to most Nigerians in my previous books but decided to revert to its official name in this book.

Therefore, I hope you will read all my previous books as referencing 'The Nigeria Police'.

WISDOM OF A SAGE

The police MUST OBEY THE LAW while

enforcing the law.

- Earl Warren

CHAPTER FIVE

THE PATHOLOGY OF POLICE RESPONSES TO CRISES AND ALLEGATIONS

As we have discussed so far, public perception is swayed partly by rumours and emotions which may not always be accurate. By and large the public may possess factual information about the police which leads to their forming a general perception about them.

But public perception can change easily and is partially dependent on the powers that control the press and media but most importantly the individual experience of each citizen that encounter the police is a dominant factor

Good experiences turn them into evangelists for the police, bad encounters make them incubators and disseminators of negative perception in the wider population.

In my opinion, the media in the Nigeria is in a very decrepit state. They have huge biases and their default prejudices are not known to many Nigerians. For instance, 80% of traditional media in Nigeria is owned by a politician or their sympathisers and surrogates.

So news coverage is always slanted, biased and prejudiced. Every story has a political slant to it. And the media has become channels for disseminating opinions and verdicts rather than simply reporting the news for Nigerians to make up their mind on the conclusion they wish.

Many undiscerning members of the public tend to believe most things they read. But the lethargy of the police in being proactive about their media engagement, has left them at the mercy of these clowns in traditional media. I have been in many police events that countless journalists will only report about if given financial incentives.

This is why the police have to develop ways of taking its message straight to the public by bypassing these newspapers and broadcasters that have made themselves roadblocks to progress. They can then in turn work with the few respectable journalist that still exist.

So this sad verdict is by no means on all the traditional media in Nigeria. There are some excellent ones but there is a big unprofessional majority that continues to do damage to the police.

This damage is done not just by constantly reporting bad news and negativity about the police; but by failing to report with the same prominence good news and positive achievements by the police.

The Pathology of Police Image Management

In trying to understand why the Nigeria police, like any organisation reacts the way it does to allegations and bad news, we will need to look into the world of organisational psychology amongst other fields for guidance. How do organisations react to a challenge to their public image the way they do?

There are many theories that could explain this situation. However, one theoretical framework is more apt that others in explaining the situation with the Nigerian police. Image restoration theory can explain a bit about how the police have been behaving and responding to negative public perceptions.

Introduced by William Benoit, image restoration theory outlines strategies that can be employed to restore image in an event where reputation has been damaged.

Image restoration theory can be applied as

an approach for understanding personal or organizational crisis situations. Benoit outlines this theory in his acclaimed book *"Accounts, Excuses, and Apologies: A Theory of Image Restoration Strategies".*[36]

This theory is based on the assumption that maintaining favourable reputation and image is the goal of an organisation. Hence how an organisation responds to news that challenges its "good image" is instructive.

Perception is fundamental to image restoration, as the accused actor will not engage in a defensive strategy unless the perception exists that he is at fault. The actor (an organisation) who committed the wrongful act must decide on the strategy of best course based on their specific situation.

Factors such as credibility, audience perceptions, and the degree of offensiveness of the act must be taken into

---

[36] Benoit, William. outlines (1995). *Accounts, Excuses, and Apologies: A Theory of Image Restoration Strategies.* New York: State University of New York Press.

account.[37]

To better understand why the police institution responds the way it does to its many critics in almost the same denial posture, Benoit's five strategic responses to crisis will help shed some light. In a summary piece, Emil B. Towner captured the essence of these strategic responses in a 2007 article.

Benoit's theory of image restoration builds upon theories of *apologia* and *accounts.* Apologia is a formal defence or justification of an individual's opinion, position, or actions,[38] and an account is a statement made by an individual or organization to explain unanticipated or transgressive events.[39]

Benoit claims that these treatments of image restoration focus on identifying options rather than prescribing solutions. He

---

[37] https://en.wikipedia.org/wiki/Image_restoration_theory
[38] Fearn-Banks, Kathleen. (2009). *Crisis Communications: A Casebook Approach*. Mahweh: Lawrence Erlbaum Associates.
[39] https://en.wikipedia.org/wiki/Image_restoration_theory

grounds image restoration theory on a comprehensive literature review of apologia and accounts theories.[40]

Based on the work done by Ware and Linkugel, William Benoit introduced perhaps the most comprehensive account of apologetic strategies in his book. Benoit's theory consists of five major strategic framework used by people or organisation who responds to accusations.
These are:
  ➢ Denial
  ➢ Evading responsibility,
  ➢ Reducing offensiveness,
  ➢ Corrective action and
  ➢ Mortification.

In addition, Benoit offers subcategories for each. According to Emil B. Towner,[41] the FIRST strategy—**Denial**—consists of two forms:
  1) **Simple denial**, in which the organisation denies the act or, at

---

[40] ibid
[41] https://emiltowner.com/2007/05/31/benoits-five-major-strategies-2/

least, denies taking part in it; or

2) **Shifting the blame**, which is also known as scapegoating. The Organisation directs the blame at someone else or to another organisation.

The SECOND strategy—**Evasion of responsibility**—consists of:

1) **Provocation**, suggesting that the organisation responded after being provoked; or that its action was in response to a wrongful act by another.

2) **Defeasibility,** suggesting that a lack of either information or control is actually to blame; pleading a lack of knowledge or control about important factors related to the offensive act.

3) **Excuses based on accidents**, suggesting it was an accident; and beyond its control.

4) **Justifies the act based on its "good intentions"**, suggesting that the

organisation performed the act with good intentions, despite the negative outcome. So it should not be held fully liable.

The THIRD strategy details how organisations attempt to **reduce the offensiveness** of their wrongful acts by using:

1) **Bolstering,** such as describing the positive attributes and qualities of the organisation in an attempt to strengthen the public's positive perception of the organisation. They may remind the public of other good acts done by the organisation in the past or is still doing.

2) **Minimization,** attempting to decrease the audience's negative view of the situation by trying to convince the public that the act in question is not as bad as it appears.

3) **Differentiation**, focusing on how a particular situation differs from similar, yet much worse acts. The hope is that the negative perception f

the public will be minimised by comparing its own action with a similar buy worse act of another organisation.

4) **Transcendence,** discussing the act in terms of abstract values and group loyalties. In this instance, the act is placed in broad context to place it in a different and less offensive frame of reference.

5) **Attacking the accuser** to undermine his or her credibility. The organisation attacks their accusers, to question the credibility of the source of the accusations.

6) **Offering compensation** to the victims. The organisation offers to redress the victims of their action to offset negative feelings towards them.

The FOURTH strategy—**Corrective action**—describes how Organisations offer to repair damages caused by their actions, as well as take steps to prevent the event from happening again.

Finally, the FIFTH strategy—**Mortification**—is based on Burke's discussion of mortification in which the accused organisation admits wrongful behaviour, takes responsibility and asks for forgiveness, and apologizes.

Practically, an organisation can employ a combination of responses in this strategy. Approach should be determined by whether the organisation is guilty of the act in question or not. A guilty organisation using the wrong strategy will do more damage to its image and credibility with the public.

The dominant recommendation is for an organization to immediately admit fault/accept responsibility. Corrective actions should be taken and an organization need to publicize those actions. Bolstering can also be thrown into the mix of responses depending on the nature of the allegation.

Denial should only be reserved for when the organisation is innocent of the allegation. If denial is used when an organisation is guilty; it tends to almost always backfire. In the case of the Nigerian police, denial does not work at all as public credibility and believability is minimal.

The Nigerian police tend to mostly deny everything. In fact, the more they deny (even if the denial is correct) the less the public seem to believe the police. So denial is causing more reputational damage to the police than if other actions had been taken.

Given the state of mistrust of the police by Nigerians, the public will initially believe any negative story about the police regardless of its authenticity. This means a lot of confidence building measure will be needed to cultivate public trust and positive perception.

The police will need to bend over backwards to be candid with Nigerians when things go wrong. Such frankness, over time will begin to impress the people to an extent that they will begin to give the police benefit of the doubt.

In another book on the police I wrote, I recommended how to reduce the political influence on the police leadership in Nigeria. This is essential because, when the police carry out unlawful order of the political leaders, they get tainted as repressive tool of the political class.

This gets them painted in the same bad brush as the politicians. Police need to begin to show itself as loyal to the constitution, law and order. This may take time but there is need for a shift in the mentality of the police leadership. Simply denying every allegation against them is not effective for the police in Nigeria.

Below are some examples of policing responses to past public accusations, just to illustrate the Benoit theory of responses.

Summary of Crisis	Benoit Strategies	Police Responses	My Analysis
National Bureau of Statistics (a government owned agency) produced a report in July 2017 that states that the police was the most corrupt agency of government based on their index.	Denial, Defeasibility	Police simply flatly disagreed with the report with no action taken based on it.	This is a missed opportunity to be candid and showcase its anti-corruption initiatives.
Sen. Misau accused the IGP and Police leadership of collecting Billion every year from the private sector for security cover provided	Denial, Attacking accuser	Police denied the allegation and then went on to attack the accuser to destroy his credibility.	The Police again missed an opportunity to win hearts and mind. Especially given the fact that most Nigerians can relate to the allegation as substantially true.

Summary of Crisis	Benoit Strategies	Police Responses	My Analysis
without declaring it.			
Reports emerged all over the media about a Payment for Promotion scandal in the Police in 2017	Denial, Evading Responsibility, Minimisation	Again the police simply denied the allegations. A compensatory step of setting up a panel to look into this lacked credibility based on the original denial.	More of the same ineffective response from the police.
Police officers were accused of letting an alleged ritual kidnapper escape in Port Harcourt after collecting bribe.	Initial denial followed by Reducing offensiveness	Initial denial of police involvement in the escape was followed by the arrest of the DPO to investigate collusion.	The right thing was done eventually in the arrest of the DPO, but final action on this may never be announced to the public. Many see it as too little too late. Although the late action was still commendable.

Even though image restoration theory represented the use of mortification (accepting responsibility) and corrective action, there might be alternative recommendations. Coombs[42] posited that there might be some alternative responses in particular situations.

In image restoration theory, Coombs argued that closer scrutiny with insights should be taken before offering strategies to crisis managers as facts.[43]

He advised that patterns should be examined to see if there are plausible responses outside of these five strategies. Detailed training and analysis on how this strategy should be deployed is beyond the scope of this book.

---

[42] Coombs, W. T. (2006). Crisis Management: A communicative approach. In C. H. Botan & V. Hazleton (Eds.), Public Relations Theory II (171-197). Mahwah, NJ: Lawrence Erlbaum Associates.
[43] ibid

WISDOM OF A SAGE

A police force, wherever they are, is made up of AMAZING PEOPLE, and I respect them a great deal.

- Nancy Mckeon

CHAPTER SIX

THE BENEFITS OF IMPROVED POLICE-COMMUNITY RELATIONS

Successful public and community engagement programs build a bridge that enables residents and law enforcement to communicate, collaborate, and work together to build safer, more caring communities.

More importantly, it opens up an otherwise insular Nigeria Police to create better empathy and understanding between Nigerians and its police institution.

A community that embraces its police and police officers that respects the community will result in better policing outcomes and enhanced collaboration.

Improved Relations allow police officers to do the following:

1) Police more effectively

2) Find their jobs safer and easier to do

3) Be treated with greater respect

4) Have better morale

5) Have more trust and less fear of police

6) Have a safer community

7) Have less tension and conflict

8) Gain greater financial and material support for the police

9) Gain quicker resolution to crime

10) Reduction in Fear of Crime.

11) Improved Police Image

Police more effectively
When trust is established between police and the community, members of the community are often more forthcoming with helpful information and potential investigative leads. Calls to the police may initially increase due to a more "open" line of communication as confidence increases.

Everyone wins when the police are able to do their jobs more effectively. There is a better information exchange and the public gain a better understanding of their police.

Police find their jobs safer and easier to do
Better community relations will make policing safer and easier to do. Public cooperation makes identifying with the police a civic duty and creates an added layer of protection for officers as the public work closer in partnership with them.

Be treated with greater respect
The respect for officers will increase as people get to understand them better. There

is nobody I have spent half an hour explaining the challenges faced by the police to that do not develop instant empathy for the police. So the more appreciation of the problem the police are facing the better respect people will have of the police. More respect for the police will change the attitude of the public when they encounter the police.

Have better Police morale

Being respected by more people in the communities is a morale booster for the police. Families of officers will be held in high esteem as well. This makes isolating the bad eggs from the force easier.

Have more trust and less fear of police

The dissipation of fear will build more trust. Securing the trust and confidence of the public is essential to deliver successful policing and law enforcement solutions anywhere in the world. A better police-public relationship will inspire worry-free encounters with the police.

Have a safer community for all

The public too often fails to realize that they must play a part in law enforcement. Their role must be active rather than passive, constructive rather than irresponsibly critical, cooperative rather than negative. So a better police-public relationship is essential to safeguard the community.

Our research indicates that procedural justice (police doing things the right way and fairly) can lead to more community cooperation — and therefore cases solved.

Improved Cooperation and have less tension and conflict

A more engaged police service will enjoy improved cooperation from the people. Stored up tension from previous bad encounters can build up to a spark that will cause community tension and conflict if not managed.

Gain greater financial and material support for the police

With better information and closer

cooperation with the police, the people will be more willing to support the police materially and financially in their communities.

Gain quicker resolution to crime

Without the cooperation of the general public, crime resolution will become an impossible task. So a better image and perception of the police will help with more reliable intelligence that will make crime resolution quicker.

Reduction in Fear of Crime.

The fear of crime is usually fuolled by people's perceived sense of safety and how rampant they feel crime is in their community. As a result, the fear of crime figures tends to be higher that the actual crime figures.

People who feel unsafe in their communities will fear more of becoming a victim of crime than those who live in relatively safe neighbourhoods. So a better relationship with the police helps to reduce the fear of crime and that is good for the police and the country.

Improved Police Image
The overall impact of better community relationship is an improved police image. Perception of the police will gradually become more positive over a period of time as the police make deliberate effort to win the heart and minds.

The "image" in this regard is the outer reflection of the standing of the police based on its performance and service. It is the reaction which emanates from the public and which is based on the public's expression of confidence and respect in a police service or a lack of such confidence and respect as the case may be.

The quality of police work must be constant. It must be emphasized again and again that public respect must not only be earned but maintained. Greater effort need to be made by the police to engage with the public and raise public affection for the Nigerian police.

Too often, people seem to forget that the policeman places his life on the line almost every time he encounters a violation of law.

Of course, we may argue, this is what he is paid for, and not one policeman will disagree with that, nor will he cry on our shoulder about it. But he does expect us to realize that police work is not a game; it is a grim and deadly business.

In the face of a rising crime rate, he asks and needs your support. I have seen many officers killed in the line of duty and it breaks my heart that the people for whom they gave their lives don't seem to appreciate the sacrifice because of the abuse of other officers.

We need to avoid throwing away the baby with the bath water so to speak. We need to support our police officers.

WISDOM OF A SAGE

When you have police officers who abuse citizens, you erode public confidence in law enforcement. That makes the job of good police officers unsafe.

- Mary Frances Berry

CHAPTER SEVEN

RECOMMENDATIONS ON HOW TO IMPROVE POLICE-PUBLIC RELATIONSHIP

There is need for a change programme within the Nigeria Police. This will be a process but it has to start from somewhere.

Putting in place a successful change strategy for the police is not an easy undertaking. It requires putting in place an integrated planning process, including steps to take before, during and after the change push.

While what you do to prepare beforehand is critical, the actions you take while implementing the change and afterwards are also very important.

Following this multi-step process can put the Nigerian Police on a path to realizing the benefits of better community relationship and citizens' appreciation.

BEFORE COMMENCING CHANGE

1. Understand previous change initiatives.
To create an effective plan, you need to know what happened during previous change initiatives (if any). That means working with stakeholders to learn what worked, what didn't and what gaps need to be filled.

2. Involve top leadership of the Police formations and State Governments.
For best success, it is imperative that senior leaders, including the state governors, are clearly behind the effort. Indeed, leaders need to drive change throughout the organization. To that end, I wish to state unequivocally that change management isn't

a "nice-to-have," but a necessity to ensure that any implementation is a success.

3. Identify people who might be potential stumbling blocks or champions.
Part of that process can involve using an assessment to help individuals understand their strengths and weaknesses. You might also ask rank and file to share the findings with the implementation team, who can help build an awareness of how they react during times of change.

How to manage those resistant to change should be agreed? Change champions should be identified and appointed from every state command and zone as well.

4. Map out a change process.
Most important is pinpointing the key areas in which officers are likely to be affected — anything from a new way of working to a reorganization of command structure—and then putting in place appropriate initiatives to help them adapt to the changes. It is also

good to consider restructuring the reward system to reinforce certain behaviours.

5. Construct an effective communications system.

The Leadership team have to communicate their vision and plan convincingly throughout the policing organization. That means building it into everything they do, from internal to external communications.

DURING AND AFTER

6. *Provide adequate support and development* for command leadership teams to lead officers through the change. That may take the form of group or one-on-one interactions, depending on the circumstances.

In some cases, it's helpful to bring command leaders together, because the process of dealing with change can be an isolating experience. At the same time, state commands should hold individual meetings with each divisional command.

7. Provide coaching for command leaders who still need help.

Provide adequate support and development to command leaders to help drive change through the policing estate. If they are unable to effectively communicate the vision and strategy and engage the rank and file through the process, the change initiative will not succeed.

State commands need to provide role clarity and ensure divisional officers are aligned with the new strategy in order to meet performance objectives and achieve goals.

8. Measure success.

Define success at the outset and the metrics to be used to assess whether leadership has achieved their goals and objectives. Success should be defined as how the institution as a whole manages change, then you might ask rank and file to fill out opinion surveys before and after the change initiative.

Without conducting an official review of the police with official support, it is not easy to fully know the esoteric internal challenges facing the Nigeria Police that will militate against progressive change.

But from my research and workings with them, the following are the salient recommendations I can make that will set them on the road to better public perception and image. But there are more recommendations that will be revealed by a future bespoke analysis work with official backing.

<u>KEY RECOMMENDATIONS</u>

My pool of recommendations will be classified to reflect the action needed to be taken by the following groups:

- **The Police Organisation.** This is the Leadership of the police led by the IGP.

- **The Police Public Relations Officers (PPRO).** Each state and zonal commands have a PPRO as well as that in the Force Headquarters. They are supposed to be the interface between the police and the media as well as the public

- **Individual Officers.** There is also a role for the individual officer.

- **The Wider Criminal Justice System.** There are duties the criminal justice system have to support the work and outcomes of policing in ways that will improve the police-public relationship.

Recommendations for the Police Organisation and Leadership

RECOMMENDATION 1:
Lead in the acceptance of Public Perception of Corruption in the Police.
You cannot change what you do not think is faulty or problematic. So, no change can take place until the police accept that they are perceived as very corrupt. This acceptance is the trigger needed to implement change and transformation.

RECOMMENDATION 2:

Institute a culture of openness with the Challenges faced by the Police.

The police need to be more candid with the public on the shortages and limitations imposed on them by their lack of resources. This candour will give the public better understanding of the challenges they face.

RECOMMENDATION 3:

Introspection and Self Analysis Exercise

There should be a **SWOT Analysis** of the Nigeria Police conducted by a team of both internal officers along with some external experts.

SWOT stands for:
- Strength
- Weakness
- Opportunities
- Threats

The SWOT should **inform certain remedial** steps to improve public perception and confidence.

RECOMMENDATION 4:
Changing Policing Philosophy
There is need for the police leadership to train officers to rethink actions to determine whether enforcement or implementing a law is really necessary. Maybe thinking twice before writing that parking ticket can help improve the community relationship.

This should also include a new strategy for Community Policing. A task force should be set up that will design a bespoke community policing format and strategy for Nigeria.

RECOMMENDATION 5:
Fear Training
Increased stress and fear training limits poor reaction errors and creates a culture of self-examination which de-escalates situations. Many reactions of the Nigerian police is as a result of misreading a situation and the danger represented by that situation. So officers shoot first out of fear.

Fear training will assist the rank and file to better analyse situations and respond more proportionately. Majority of the police shootings in Nigeria involve people who are not armed. This should not be happening at the rate in which it occurs.

But retraining the brain, repairing biases, rethinking the real role of a police officer and changing the law enforcement culture will take time. But it has to start somehow and from somewhere. So why not now?

RECOMMENDATION 6:
Enable Officers to live in the community they Protect
The more officers live in the communities they protect, the better their community relationship which prevents and solves crimes.

The police leadership should provide the necessary structure and funding to help officers live in their own communities rather than in barracks. The more normal interactions officers have with their communities the better for the image of the police.

RECOMMENDATION 7:

Openness with the material help and support given to the police by non-Federal Government bodies

If the people know the full scale of the needs of the police that are not covered through federal funding, they will better appreciate the constraints officers work under.

Hence, openness by the police on the scale of the support it gets from all and sundry will help embarrass the government into action so to speak. A better appreciation of the challenges facing the police can only strengthen the empathy for the police and foster better relationship and cooperation.

RECOMMENDATION 8:

Invest in more Crime-Prevention Initiatives

If the only time the public interact with the police is always after a crime has been committed; then the view of the police will be skewed. More low-level interaction that is of advisory and consultative nature helps police image to improve.

RECOMMENDATION 9:

Internal Communication Enhancement

There must be a way for the IGP to communicate certain things internally & directly to all officers without any managerial or command filter. Like the Chinese Whispers, many things are lost in translation when superior officers disseminate orders given from above. Rank and file end up hearing different versions of the same instruction.

While this cannot replace normal command-directed briefings; a system should be put in place that will allow the IGP to communicate with all officers on critical matters or updates. This will help ensure uniformity of the nature and context of strategic information.

RECOMMENDATION 10:

More recruitment of Female officers

Female officers are generally seen as less threatening by the public. So they can be great ambassadors for the police. Police aggression is a guy thing. Most police shootings are by male officers. In fact, I do not have a record of a female officer shooting a member of the public. There may have been but I have not found any information of it. Female officers are generally less aggressive. Their presence help tamp down some of that male testosterone that lead to excesses.

The police leadership should encourage the recruitment of more female officers even if a target has to be imposed for short time to drive up the percentages.

RECOMMENDATION 11:
Invest heavily in ongoing training of the Rank and File
Training is one of the things the police seem to pay lip service to. I have met Deputy Commissioners of Police in state commands who are in charge of training but have no team and have not conducted any training for many years. This post appears to be ok on paper but there are no resources and hardly do they conduct any training.

There has to be a rule that every officer must

attend training annually. Even if it is a two-day training seminar in an area of operation. Better training for the police workforce will improve behaviour, change policing paradigm, identify bad habits that need to be changed and ultimately improve community perception.

RECOMMENDATION 12:
Make Police Officers and their good work more Visible
As part of a form of community policing, there need to be better visibility for the police in various communities. Many criminals will be deterred by the mere fact that a police team may be on a street any moment doing their normal daily patrol. This gives the public more confidence in the police.

RECOMMENDATION 13:
Be more willing to apologise and take responsibility for mistakes.
Nobody expects the police to be perfect. None are anywhere in the world. Be willing to admit your mistakes. This will endear you

to the public even more than denials that can be easily discounted as untrue.

RECOMMENDATION 14:
Investigate all fatal police shootings (Good or Bad) and report them promptly to the people.
All fatal police shootings should be investigated to show the public you take seriously any loss of life. Lessons learnt should be publicised.

RECOMMENDATION 15:
Explore the widespread use of non-lethal weapons, thus making lethal ones a last resort.
The Nigeria Police should explore the use of non-lethal weapons and deploy these to officers. This will allow low level threats to be neutralised without any loss of life. Fewer cases of police killing definitely help improve the image of the police.

RECOMMENDATION 16:

Quarterly Reports should be produced and Town Hall meetings should become regular across the communities in various State Commands.

There should be periodic meetings with the public at either zonal or state command level as well as nationally.

This will look engaging, consultative and accountable. This will involve Questions and answers sessions as well as reports to the public including updates on all pertinent matters and investigations.

RECOMMENDATION 17:

Force Headquarters should create a role of **Social Media Officer** *(if non exist), within each zone who will in turn liaise with states within each zone.*

There should be a designated individual in each zone who will be responsible for social media management on a day to day basis.

This does not have to be a uniformed officer. So an administrative employee can do the role.

RECOMMENDATION 18:
A Social Media Strategy document should be created for the Nigeria Police collectively and a version can then be tweaked for each zone.
There should be an agreed media engagement strategy for the Nigerian police as relating to both traditional and social media. But this must be based on a Social Media strategy nationally approved. A sample methodology for producing this strategy is included in Appendix 2.

Recommendations for the Police Public Relations Offices

RECOMMENDATION 19:
The PPRO function should be professionalized.
I am less concerned whether the occupier is a serving officer or not. But they should be trained in the art of Public Relations and

Media management. This should not be a role that just any officer can be transferred into to perform. It is good to see the policed have established a Public Relations school. This is a step in the right direction.

RECOMMENDATION 20:
The use of Social Media should be a compulsory tool by the PPROs.
This requires each state command to have a comprehensive Media (including Social Media) Strategy. Social media success is less about quantity and more about the quality of engagement between citizens and the police.

There should be an active Social media contact channel for each PPRO in the country.

To proactively shape sentiment, police organisations must tailor their engagement efforts to different community segments using a variety of channels and recognise that one size does not fit all.

RECOMMENDATION 21:

The police social media handles must never be personalised.

All police social media handles and hashtags must remain official and not be personalised to the name of any individual officer. This helps to maintain brand consistency for the police.

It will be confusing to the public if social media names or handles change every time the officer in charge is redeployed to other duties. PPROs must not be allowed to promote personal social media postings while in the role. Only the official command level social media postings and hashtags should be promoted.

RECOMMENDATION 22:

Commit to a Doctrine of Honesty.

To maintain credibility, encourage your superiors to understand that it is better not to say anything at all than to lie to the public.

So discourage yourself from holding press statement if your plan or instruction is to lie to the people. Your words need to be presumed honest unless proven otherwise.

Recommendations for Individual Police Officers

RECOMMENDATION 23:

Presentation is King. Officers must ensure they look their best at all time.

Several research studies have shown that people love and obey more officers who are smartly dressed and neat than scruffy dressing and dirty appearances. So as part of your duty to maintain a positive image of the police, individual officers need to dress presentably at all times on duty.

RECOMMENDATION 24:

Act as though you are being recorded at all times.

Officers should always behave and respond to situations as though they are being recorded and will be put on social media. What you will be ashamed for the world to see that you are doing, you must not do at all. Always be conscious of your duty to help maintain a positive image of the police.

Recommendations for the wider Criminal Justice System.

RECOMMENDATION 25:
Creation of a Joint working team on Speedy Justice.
Police raising their game will affect the wider criminal justice system like the courts and prisons. So a new working group should be created involving these departments to focus on Speedy Justice strategy that will help boost confidence in the entire justice system. This will collaterally impact all the players in the justice landscape.

COMMENTS ON ONGOING OR RECENT DEVELOPMENTS

Police Complaint Rapid Response Unit (PCRRU) not working.
While I support the creation of a complaints handling mechanism by the police, the PCRRU is ill thought through and not

effectively managed. If the reasons for the public reluctance to report crimes to the police is not addressed why would the same people voluntarily contact the police complaints unit?

There are also many weaknesses in the way this unit is being managed and I do not wish to give free consulting review in this book on this. But one of the basics they are getting wrong is for instance their engagement with the social media.

Their Twitter handle for example excessively promotes the personal postings of its head. This is wrong. What happens when the leadership is changed? All the threads will be lost and media recognition established will vanish. An official Twitter handle such as *#PoliceComplaints* or something similar (which I know already exists) will create continuity regardless of who the head is. But promoting personal names on the Twitter handle is not a good move and also makes quick recognition or affiliation to the police more difficult to establish.

Military on the Streets

As at September 2017, the Nigerian Military is on active deployment in 28 states. This should be a worrisome development as the police are the leading agency in civil enforcements.

Other than the North Eastern states where the Boko Haram insurgency is being fought, the military should be in their barracks. The military who are supposed to be last resort are now routine. Could this routine deployment of the military be as a result of a crisis of confidence in the police? Or could the federal government be breaking the law with these deployments.

Regardless of the motive, such massive deployment undermines the police in the eyes of the public and as such should be stopped. The police should be strengthened and resourced to do its constitutional duties instead of being bypassed on a large scale like this.

The police if trained and equipped can become the pride of this nation so the government should desist from acts that can unwittingly undermine public support for it. The Police should be in charge of all civil acts of public protection, unless in the extreme cases when they will have to call in the military for support.

FINALLY
Effective policing demands public trust and engagement. Gaining that trust and engagement goes beyond reducing crime levels, but also preventing crime in the first place.

Policing is about people and the Nigerian police must understand that without public support, they cannot function effectively. So a new paradigm is needed to develop a new culture of policing in Nigeria that will serve our people better and achieve greater outcomes.

It is my hope that this book has helped you better appreciate not only the challenges facing the police, but how the public see the police. I hope the recommendations in this book will be looked at seriously and implemented for the sake of a more effective law enforcement landscape.

APPENDIX 1

PRINCIPLES OF CRIME PREVENTION

Preventing crime is:[44]

- **Everyone's business**. Crime prevention is not just the business of law enforcement. Law enforcement alone cannot prevent crime. It takes concerned citizens of all ages to prevent and reduce crime.

- **More than security.** Prevention of crime addresses a broad range of issues that affect the quality of life of

---

[44] curled from www.ncpc.org

the community and all its members. Crime prevention works best when it embraces both the physical and the human environment, when it seeks not just to reduce risk but to reduce the conditions that cause risk.

- **A responsibility at all levels and agencies of government.** Prevention is a sound government investment. Agencies within each level of government, not just law enforcement, have a stake in promoting crime prevention.

- **Linked with solving social problems.** Crime is caused in part by social problems that permeate all aspects of society. Some examples of this include poverty, lack of education, substance abuse, and unemployment. Problem-solving approaches to policing have highlighted the need to address community structural and social issues to restore order, reduce fear, and curb crime.

- **Cost-effective.** Research has increasingly documented that well-designed, well-managed crime prevention initiatives can more than pay for themselves. Crime is expensive in financial, physical, and psychological costs to the victim; in addition, the costs of crime include policing; the investigation, arrest, trial, and sentencing; and the lost productivity of individuals and businesses, not to mention the costs of the social disorder and isolation that result from crime or fear of crime.

Preventing crimes require:

- **A central role in law enforcement.** Law enforcement needs community support. Community residents and leaders need to support prevention

- **Cooperation and collaboration by all elements of the community.** Effective crime prevention for the neighbourhood or community requires a process of identifying and solving problems, taking immediate steps to improve safety, developing conditions that forestall problems, and determining the future direction the community needs to take. The best way to do this is to form some type of crime prevention group like a Coalition, Homeowners Association, etc.

- **Education**. Education is at the core of crime prevention. It embraces information, training, and motivation to action at all levels. It helps all residents of our communities make themselves and their homes safer. It informs and engages all government agencies.

- **Tailoring to local needs and conditions.** Crime prevention strategies and programs that have proved effective, especially those at the local level, can be used by other communities facing similar needs and concerns. Programs must be transferred with appropriate adjustments and adaptations. No two communities are alike, and successful programs recognize and compensate for these differences.

- **Continual testing and improvement.** Document the effectiveness of crime prevention programs and strategies. Be alert to local, national, and international trends. Measure performance and assess outcomes. Seek and expand commitment from the entire community.

APPENDIX 2[45]

SOCIAL MEDIA AND TACTICAL CONSIDERATIONS FOR LAW ENFORCEMENT – A Western Police Case Study[46]

INTRODUCTION

The 21st century is becoming known as an Age of Technology, and one of the most important and complex types of new technology is social media.

At its core, social media is a tool for communication that has become an integral part of daily life for people of all ages.

Social media accounts for 22 percent of time

---

[45] Some of the contents in this Appendix will not apply to the Nigerian Police as it is an American document. But key elements of it can be used to produce a bespoke document for the NPF.
[46] Curled from a publication by the Office of Community Oriented Policing Services, U.S. Department of Justice. 2013.

- 183 -

spent on the Internet,[47] and even among people age 65 and older—who are not generally considered prime users of new technologies—one in four people are now active on a social media website. Facebook claimed to have 955 million monthly active users worldwide at the end of June 2012.[48]

Law enforcement agencies, like many other types of organizations, are finding ways to use social media to disseminate information to the public. In fact, police agencies in larger cities are finding that their communities expect them to have an online presence on platforms such as Twitter, Facebook, and YouTube.

Police departments also have begun to explore the use of social media to obtain information, especially for tactical purposes, such as gathering information about threats of mob violence, riots, or isolated criminal activity during otherwise-lawful mass demonstrations.

Social media has now given protesters the ability to informally and very quickly organize

---

[47]   See   http://blog.nielsen.com/nielsenwire/global/social-media-accounts-for-22-percent-of-time-online/.
[48] See http://newsroom.fb.com/content/default.aspx?NewsAreaId=22.

and communicate with each other in real time. Police must know how to monitor these types of communications in order to gauge the mood of a crowd, assess whether threats of criminal activity are developing, and stay apprised of any plans by large groups of people to move to other locations.

Similarly, in the aftermath of an incident of mob violence, police can "mine" social networking sites to identify victims, witnesses, and perpetrators. Witnesses to crime—and even perpetrators—often post photographs, videos, and other information about an incident that can be used as investigative leads or evidence.

Police agencies must also consider how their own actions are reported to the public through social media. Nearly any action taken in public by a police officer may be recorded on a mobile device and instantly uploaded to YouTube or another social networking site. Many of today's police chiefs have said that they generally advise their officers to always behave in public as if they are being recorded, because that very well may be the case.

Another consideration is that crime victims and witnesses can quickly transmit information about a crime scene or criminal act out to the world, impeding a detective's ability to control the release of information about a case.

The strategic challenges of monitoring social networks and transforming huge amounts of data into actionable intelligence can be a daunting task for police agencies. But this is an achievable task.

The use of social media in policing is an issue that has only begun to emerge in the last few years, so policy appears to be lagging behind practice to some extent.

Developing a Strategy on Social Media
Many police departments have begun to use social media in tentative or experimental ways. But because the social media phenomenon is relatively new, many police agencies have not yet taken a more comprehensive approach to considering their overall philosophy and approach toward social networking.

The Toronto Police Service (TPS) has a reputation in the field as one of the most advanced law enforcement agencies in the use of social media. There are currently over 200 individuals in the TPS who have received training and are authorized to use social media to communicate on behalf of the department.[49]

Following is an account of TPS's early initiatives with social media, dating as far back as 2007, as well as TPS's development of a comprehensive social media strategy in 2010–2011.

One Agency's Experience: THE TORONTO POLICE SERVICE

Social media and communications technology companies have become an important part of the Toronto-area economy in recent years, to the extent that there has been some discussion of whether Toronto should aim to become a "Silicon Valley of the North." So it was no surprise to many members of the

---

[49] Readers are encouraged to view the TPS Social Media page at www.torontopolice.on.ca/socialmedia/ for links to the Twitter, Facebook, and YouTube pages of many TPS employees across the department.

Toronto Police Service when residents began to have extended communications on social networking sites about public safety issues.

A few young police officers and supervisors recognized the need for TPS to participate in certain online conversations, particularly with regard to crime prevention and traffic issues, and they didn't want the agency to miss a potentially valuable opportunity.

"EARLY ADOPTERS" OF SOCIAL MEDIA WITHIN THE POLICE SERVICE

Constable Scott Mills, an officer in TPS's Public Information Unit, was one of the first officers to bring social media to the attention of his supervisors. Constable Mills was involved in the Toronto Crime Stoppers program, a 25-year-old organization of concerned citizen volunteers who solicit information and tips on crime from the community. Crime Stoppers uses traditional media outlets such as posters, television public service announcements, billboards, and newspaper features to gather information.

In 2007, Constable Mills began to feel that TPS was "missing the boat" on social media. According to Chief William Blair, Mills understood that many of the people whom Crime Stoppers wanted to reach didn't watch the local six o'clock news or read newspapers. Instead, young people with information about crime in the community were getting and sharing news and information via social media platforms and other Internet-based sources.

Constable Mills posted the first Crime Stoppers video on YouTube in April 2007, launching a new way for Crime Stoppers to connect with the public. Chief Blair admitted to having some reservations about using YouTube, but he agreed to the initial posting, and the public response was overwhelmingly positive. The number of tips coming in to TPS increased exponentially.[50] Following the YouTube campaign, Toronto Crime Stoppers created a Facebook page and a Twitter account.

---

[50] "How Constable Scott Mills's social media work protects Toronto." Digital Journal, Sept. 16, 2010. http://digitaljournal.com/article/297670.

Sergeant Tim Burrows, an officer in TPS's Traffic Unit, saw how successful social media was with Toronto Crime Stoppers, and began using it in the Traffic Unit in 2009. Burrows noticed that Toronto residents were using social media to post their "pet peeves" and other information about traffic-related issues.

Burrows began to actively participate in the discussions, using Twitter, Facebook, and YouTube to reach out to the community, offer information, answer questions, and discuss traffic and road safety issues.

Developing a Comprehensive Strategy

By 2010, TPS Deputy Chief Peter Sloly was noticing the early efforts at bringing social media to the Police Service, and he recognized that there was a need for a larger, more structured approach. He attended the first international "SMILE" conference (Social Media, the Internet, and Law Enforcement), held in Washington, D.C., in April of that year.

Taking a devil's advocate approach, Deputy Chief Sloly brought a group of officers to the conference who he believed would be able to identify risks or potential problems with using social media in a police agency. But after attending the conference, he said, the officers saw the potential benefits and did not try to convince him or TPS Chief William Blair to step back from social media.

Sloly obtained Chief Blair's approval to undertake a comprehensive project to develop a TPS "corporate strategy." As the director of the project, Sloly organized a working group of TPS officers as well as a contractor with expertise in social media in a law enforcement environment, LAwS Communications, which was the organization that held the SMILE conference.

Sloly, the working group, and the contractor then developed a strategy for achieving wide-ranging goals for social media within TPS. These included creating policies to ensure "sound governance" in the ways in which TPS officers post information or otherwise use social media, developing a training module for officers who are chosen to engage in social media, finding ways to use social media to improve communications within TPS as well as communications to the public, and creating a plan to measure whether social media efforts are effective.

These efforts culminated in the official launch of TPS's social media program on July 27, 2011. That day, the first class of TPS employees who had completed a newly developed social media training course was given authorization to represent the department via social media. Since that time, scores of additional officers have completed the training and have launched Twitter or Facebook accounts to communicate about issues in their sphere of influence.

Chief Blair and Deputy Chief Sloly have discussed a number of general guiding principles for social media in policing. They emphasize that while social media is a useful tool for communication, its use must ultimately support TPS's goal of fighting crime.

"Social media is not a silver bullet," Sloly said. "It enables us to do old business in newer ways, but we still have to do old business."

And from the beginning, TPS has emphasized two-way communications between officers and the public. Social media should not be just another "megaphone" for the police to spread their messages; it should be used to solicit communications from the public to the police as well, Sloly said.

One important element of the TPS strategy is that in many cases, TPS officers who see a role for social media in their jobs have been allowed to "self-select"—asking to undergo the social media training, and develop their own TPS social media profiles. It is important to note that these are not personal social media accounts, but rather official TPS accounts.

In the early years of social media, TPS's focus was on using social media externally, to communicate with the public. But under the comprehensive strategy, TPS is working to improve internal department communications using social media platforms as well.

Social media facilitates communications between members of the department, independent of rank structures and chain of command. For example, Deputy Chief Sloly maintains a visible command-level presence online, directly communicating with officers— commenting on items they post on Facebook, retweeting their Twitter posts, and linking with them on LinkedIn.

As the use of social media for communications increased within the TPS, crime-fighting applications became apparent. Detectives began to look at social networking communications produced by persons of interest in their criminal investigations.

And when large-scale, high-profile events have taken place in Toronto (e.g., the 2010 G20 Summit and Occupy Toronto protests), the agency's experience with social media platforms made it nimbler in reading and understanding protesters' social media communications, in order to identify potential problems or clear up miscommunications between the police and the public.

One social media-related issue that emerged from the 2010 working group discussions was "cyber-vetting" of potential TPS employees— i.e., evaluating job candidates' online presence and reputation. Because police employees must be trustworthy, candidates may be unsuitable if they have posted comments or other content on social media sites that is perceived as damaging to the trust that a police department must earn with the public.

For example, obscene, racist, or reckless comments made by a job candidate on Facebook or Twitter can disqualify candidates or raise serious questions about their judgment and character.

A TPS sub-group worked on this issue and produced several pages of policy and guidance on cyber-vetting, based in part on a policy guide published by the International Association of Chiefs of Police (IACP).[51]

The TPS policy provides that cyber-vetting may be conducted only by certain designated TPS employees. The purposes of cyber-vetting are to verify information provided by the candidate at other stages of the application

---

[51] www.theiacp.org/PublicationsGuides/ResearchCenter/Publications/t abid/299/Default.aspx?id=1333&v=1.

process, to identify candidates who have posted material that indicates involvement in or association with criminal activity or individuals, and to identify candidates whose online behaviour goes against TPS's core values.

The policy provides that candidates should not be asked for their passwords to social media sites, and cyber searches will not unlawfully bypass candidates' privacy settings on social media sites.

Ensuring Quality Control in Social Media

TPS's Corporate Communications unit helps to guide the scores of TPS personnel who communicate on behalf of the agency via social media platforms. For example, the Corporate Communications unit has issued a one-page guide with basic tips, including the following:

> ➢ **"Your accounts are yours but they represent us.** You are free to comment and speak on matters that you have an expertise or working knowledge of, but you are not official spokespersons of the Service..."

> ➢ **"The Internet is forever.** Search engines, screen capturing,…and other technologies make it virtually impossible to take something back. Be sure of what you mean to say, and say what you mean."
> ➢ **"Be sensitive to the privacy of others and the Service.** Do not share any information of others including their photos without their permission…."
> ➢ **"Treat others as you want to be treated.** Always be respectful and patient with others."

The Corporate Communications unit informally monitors communications on TPS social media accounts in order to ensure that TPS officers are maintaining high standards of quality and are adhering to the Service's guidelines.

The Corporate Communications unit also keeps an eye on what members of the public are saying about the Police Service. Only publicly available communications are observed. With the exception of several low-cost or free programs (e.g., Radian6 or

TweetDeck), no specialized equipment is used for this monitoring. Typically, the comments and conversations that concern TPS are about high-profile criminal cases and incidents involving the police.

Communications are sometimes reviewed to gauge the public mood, particularly following specific incidents that may lead to anti-police sentiment.

According to Director of Corporate Communications Mark Pugash, if a TPS employee makes an inappropriate statement or commits some other error, it is important to monitor the public reaction in order to ensure that TPS can respond quickly and directly.

It can be effective to respond in the online forums where an incident is already being discussed, rather in other venues that may not reach the persons who are most concerned about an incident. In some cases, there may be false or misleading statements about the TPS that online responses can help to correct.

TPS also has expanded its analysis of social media during large events and mass demonstrations. During the 2010 G8 and G20 Summits in Toronto, TPS used two officers on 12-hour shifts to analyse public opinion and communications by protesters.

A review of keywords and hash-tags showed that the citizens more frequently used Twitter as they sought information about road closures, mass transit disruptions, and police and demonstrator movements. Those posting negative comments about the police used Facebook more frequently than other social media platforms.

At one point, TPS had to shut down the ability of people to post comments on TPS's main Facebook wall, because the Service was unable to keep up with the large quantity of posts.

Like many police agencies, TPS posts "Terms of Use" for its Facebook pages, stating that TPS may remove viewer comments that are racist, defamatory, threatening, obscene, or otherwise "inappropriate or offensive."

(Managing viewer comments on a police department Facebook page can be a difficult issue. The Honolulu Police Department changed its Facebook posting policy to an open-posting rule after litigants claimed in a federal lawsuit that the department deleted posts that were unfavourable to the department.

During the 2011 Occupy Toronto protests, on several occasions TPS responded to false online allegations that the police were storming the Occupy camp or taking other action against the group. Social media was used to reassure and educate the public.

Because social media is used extensively by organizers and participants in major protests and other large events, TPS is exploring the possibility of having a social media commander at such events, whose presence in the command centre would allow the police to respond more quickly to changing developments.

Training

TPS conducts two distinct training sessions that cover issues related to social media. The first is a three-day course about the use of social media by members of the Toronto Police Service to communicate with and engage the public.

The second course is a comprehensive five-day training session offered to investigators regarding a variety of computer-facilitated crimes, investigative strategies, and use of social media in criminal investigations.

Training Course on Communicating with the Public: The first training course, developed as part of TPS's 2011 social media strategy, is conducted by personnel from the Corporate Communications unit. The course is believed to be unique among Canadian police agencies, and TPS has received requests from other agencies seeking to send representatives to the training. (As of this writing, limits on resources have prevented TPS from making the course available to other agencies.)

Selection of TPS employees for the course is based on a unit commander's careful assessment of whether an individual is a good candidate to serve as a public voice of the TPS. This is based partly on the candidate's understanding of the concepts of risk management and professionalism.

As in other types of organizations, there are certain members of police departments who lack the perspective and judgment to speak on behalf of TPS in such a highly visible way.

The Corporate Communications staff also realized early on that if a police employee lacks enthusiasm about social media or lacks a strong desire to engage people online, that employee should not be given a role in social media. Such an employee would consider social media duties just another task to perform, and would quickly grow weary of it.

The first day of class provides an introduction to the TPS social media project, so trainees will understand the considerations made by the agency as it established its social media policy and training.

Social media and professional standards are discussed in the context of the overall corporate communications plan for TPS. Participants are given examples of how to effectively communicate to the public through original outgoing messaging, by leveraging other online information sources, and through responses to incoming messages from the public.

The second and third days of training are held in a computer lab, and participants create user accounts that are compliant with TPS standards.

Users are provided with basic tutorials on the two most commonly used social media sites, Facebook and Twitter. A good portion of one day is spent learning about Facebook security settings. Participants are also provided with electronic versions of TPS logos, disclosure statements, and other guidance to promote uniformity of appearance in all TPS-sponsored accounts.

Training Course on Computer-Facilitated Crime and Investigative Strategies:

An experienced cybercrime detective leads a five-day training course in computer-facilitated crime for investigators. The course is designed for division-level detectives, but not for persons involved in covert or undercover assignments. The course topics include:

> ➢ Internet investigations, including IP addresses and tracing websites
> ➢ Social media searches and source intelligence
> ➢ Facebook account management, privacy settings, and data searches
> ➢ Cellular telephones and devices, Internet service providers, and cell tower data
> ➢ Search and seizure of computers, cell phones, and related devices
> ➢ Forensic analysis of computers, cell phones, and related devices
> ➢ Cross-border investigations, multi-agency cooperation, and other law enforcement resources
> ➢ eLearning tools and resources for continuing education

Strategies and Lessons Learned

➢ Do not allow an over-sensitivity to risk assessment to derail the process of developing social media. There will always be individuals in any organization who focus on the potential pitfalls of a new technology or process. Police leaders should focus on the potential rewards of using social media and then work to mitigate risks.

➢ Keep your policy clear and the language simple. As with the creation of other types of policy, it was vital to TPS to involve all relevant stakeholders in the creation of its social media strategy. Model policies are helpful starting points, but TPS stressed that customization is important. Policy-makers should ensure that use of social media complies with local, state/territory, and federal laws, as well as with the user agreements of the social media providers.

➢ Identify the right people to use social media. Police agencies should carefully consider whom they want to empower to take visible public roles for the organization. Not everyone is a "natural" at speaking and writing clearly, with sensitivity to political and social issues and other considerations. However, training can help many people improve their skills in this area. If you choose the right people, they will view social media as an integral part of their position, not as a time-consuming add-on to existing duties.

Although most people with an interest in taking a social media role will already be familiar with the basics of Facebook, Twitter, and other media, be prepared to train your people on the context of their use. Talk with your officers to see what they may already be doing with social media and ask how they might do it better with agency support.

FINALLY
Determine whether your policy must cover potential misuse of social media. Early on, the TPS decided that it did not need to address issues of misconduct in its social media policy.

Misconduct, including disclosure of confidential information and failing to represent the department in a professional manner, is already covered in other policies.

Problems may occur less often than you expect, Deputy Chief Peter Sloly indicated. "Our people are more professional and better communicators than we tend to give them credit for," he said.

He also pointed out that misconduct committed via social media can be easier to investigate than other types of misconduct, because social media postings are recorded. There is automatically a record of the act of misconduct or potential misconduct, making investigations more
clear-cut.

Determine where you want to begin with your strategy. If your department is new to social media, it may make sense to begin a social media program internally. Teach your personnel to use their social networking skills internally and then advance to external communications and a community-focused program.

Bringing in a social media expert as a consultant may help to give the program credibility in the eyes of your officers and the public.

Decide who will be in charge of social media in your agency. Some departments may develop social media in the divisions or units with the most direct and visible community interactions (e.g., patrol, crime prevention, traffic, and school resource officers). Others may restrict official postings in social media to members of the public information and communications unit.

TPS warned against placing a social media coordinator within every unit or patrol division, saying that instead, there should be one central communications strategy, to include social media communications, for the entire department.

See the full potential of social media across the police department. Social media should not be seen merely as a tool for improved "corporate communications," in the view of Toronto Deputy Chief Sloly.

"Rather, social media should be mainstreamed into all operations, from crime prevention to intelligence gathering, from next-generation computer-aided dispatch to criminal investigations, public order management, and community policing," he said. "It also must become one of the main Information Technology tools for reducing costs and improving public values in areas like human resources, professional standards/risk management, finance and administration, information management, performance management, and public/private partnerships.

As of 2012, the Toronto Police has social media applications in all these areas. Social media and digital platforms are transforming the private/public sectors of society. Police leaders can and must embrace social media and use it to help transform policing in order to keep pace with society."

BOOKS BY DR CHARLES OMOLE

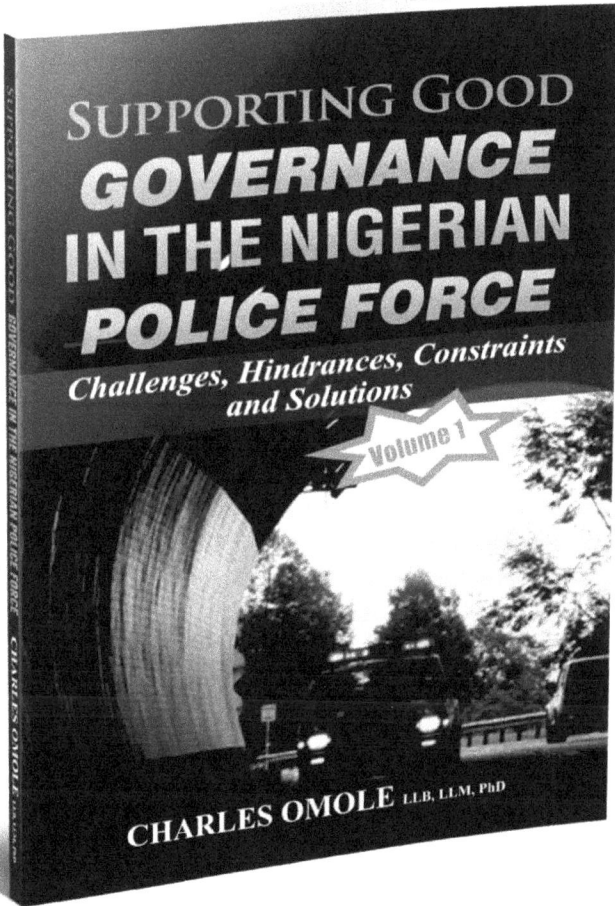

SUPPORTING GOOD GOVERNANCE IN THE NIGERIAN POLICE FORCE

Challenges, Hindrances, Constraints and Solutions

Volume 1

CHARLES OMOLE LLB, LLM, PhD

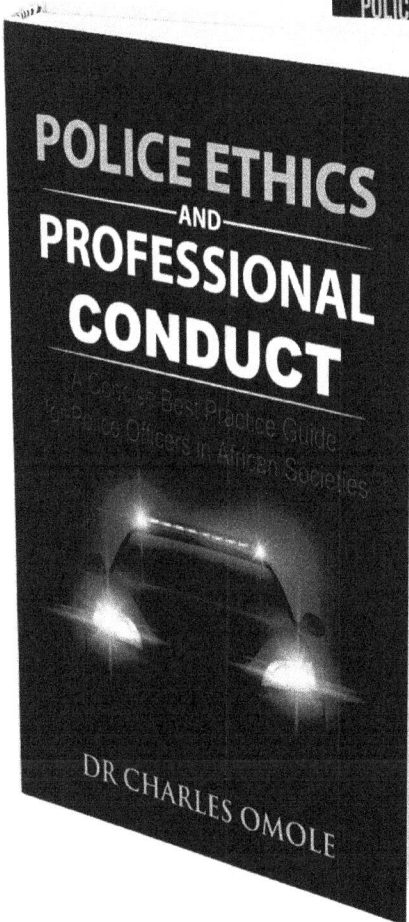

POLICE ETHICS
—AND—
PROFESSIONAL
CONDUCT

A Concise Best Practice Guide
for Police Officers in African Societies

DR CHARLES OMOLE

POLICE ETHICS AND PROFESSIONAL C

cal dilemmas every day in the cour
cal conundrums and challenges evolve
is no static right or wrong ways of de
ver exist a range of acceptable re
your knowledge, exposure and train
the best possible chance of making th
ed on new developments and thinking
This book provides all the details you
n. The goal isn't to make everyone the
aking. Ethics is not an underhanded att
you; you can only change yourself. Eth
ics are flawed. This isn't remedial ethic
e learn to make the best choices and c
f policing in African societies.

at ethics is a perishable skill. It is a ski
updated. It requires continual training
. The more updated you are, the bett
as a police officer. This book present
w enforcement with a concise, yet det
ce work, how to deal with ethical dilem
andard of professional conduct as po
also reflects the peculiarities of Afric
echanisms in situational ethical scenari

es Omole is a lawyer, consultan
nts across the globe and also a co
e brings together an excellent acc
and practical industry experience as
g proposition. He has managed o
ation programme budgets over the p
the globe. He received his LLB at t
. Through his research he obtained
ing Jurisprudence. Dr Omole also
rship and Administration. He desig
cement agencies across the world. He
versatile depth of
him a formidable
ught after adviser

ISBN 978-1

9 781907

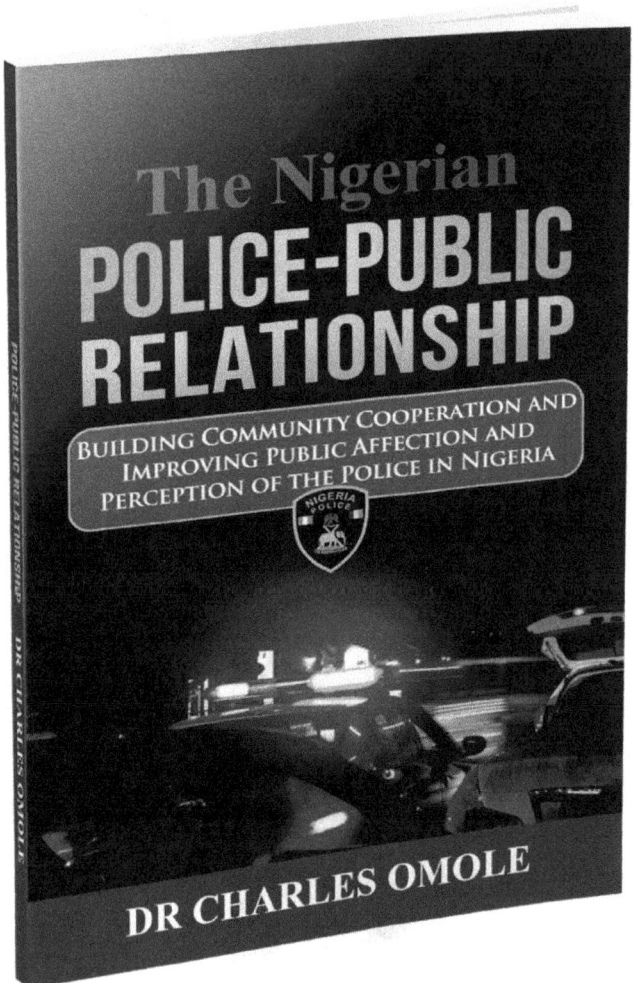

CONTACT DETAILS

Dr. Charles Omole can be reached on:

Charlesomole@gmail.com

NOTES

www.ingramcontent.com/pod-product-compliance
Lightning Source LLC
Chambersburg PA
CBHW060015210326
41520CB00009B/898